|| -

a Sunday Times series (No. 81)

Handbook for the

TRIUMPH
1300 and 1300 TC

from 1965

– –

PIET OLYSLAGER MSIA MSAE

NELSON

THOMAS NELSON AND SONS LTD
36 Park Street London W1
P.O. Box 2187 Accra
P.O. Box 336 Apapa Lagos
P.O. Box 25012 Nairobi
P.O. Box 21149 Dar es Salaam
77 Coffee Street San Fernando Trinidad

THOMAS NELSON (AUSTRALIA) LTD
597 Little Collins Street Melbourne

THOMAS NELSON AND SONS (CANADA) LTD
81 Curlew Drive Don Mills Ontario

THOMAS NELSON AND SONS (SOUTH AFRICA) (PTY) LTD
51 Commissioner Street, Johannesburg

THOMAS NELSON AND SONS
Copewood and Davis Streets Camden New Jersey 08103

17—160081—9

English language edition

© OLYSLAGER ORGANISATION N.V. 1968

Printed in Gt. Britain by GALLEON PRINTERS LIMITED, HAZEL GROVE, CHESHIRE

iv

Contents

(for Triumph 1300 TC see page 66)

SPECIAL NOTE

Preface

THIS MANUAL is intended to supplement (not to replace) the instruction book issued with the vehicle by the manufacturer. It contains more detailed information on the maintenance and repair of the Triumph 1300 without being, or pretending to be, a fully comprehensive workshop manual.

The first sections of the book contain general information essential for both owner-driver and mechanic. They give full details about the models covered so that the reader does not have to refer to many different publications in order to find correct model designations, serial numbers, major modifications, prices, dimensions, lubrication, maintenance and other information.

The section 'Repair Data' has been compiled and presented on the assumption that the reader knows something about repair work. Elementary procedures have therefore been omitted and the space has been devoted to more advanced information. Readers who are not qualified to carry out repairs and adjustments are strongly advised to leave them to Standard-Triumph dealers or distributors whose mechanics possess special equipment and are fully informed about the latest modifications and design changes. Often it will be more economical to replace a component by either a new or a factory-reconditioned unit rather than attempt to repair it. In all cases of doubt it will pay to consult a dealer.

All the important dimensions, tolerances and other specifications are presented in convenient tabular form at the end of the book, followed by an engine fault-finding chart.

PIET OLYSLAGER, MSIA, MSAE

Fig. 1. Triumph 1300 four-door Saloon, three-quarter front view

Fig. 2. Triumph 1300 four-door Saloon, three-quarter rear view

TRIUMPH 1300* from 1965

General

INTRODUCTION

The Triumph 1300, a product of the Standard-Triumph Motor Company Ltd., was announced by Standard-Triumph International Ltd. on 15 October, 1965, and first publicly shown at the Earls Court Motor Show in London.

Deliveries, however, did not commence until January 1966.

The new 1300, Series RD, or 'Ajax' as it had been known throughout its development period, is a front-wheel drive, four-door, luxurious but compact saloon with a four-cylinder 1296cc engine and many interesting and some revolutionary features.

The first prototype 'Ajax' was produced in 1963/64 and series production commenced early in August 1965. Between then and January 1966, 200 cars were allocated to a cross-section of potential owners for testing purposes. Minor faults discovered during the course of these tests resulted in modifications which were carried out on all cars before they were sold to the public.

The 1300 TC model is a twin-carburettor higher performance version of the 1300 saloon and was introduced on 3 October 1967. This model is dealt with in a special supplement on page 66.

DESCRIPTION

The Triumph 1300, like the larger 2000 models, was styled by the Italian designer Giovanni Michelotti, and is equipped with a unique engine/transmission unit. The engine itself is a larger-capacity version of the well-proven 1200 ohv power unit (as used in the Herald and Spitfire models) with a piston displacement of 1296cc, developing 61 bhp at 5000 rpm. Carburation is by a single side-draught Stromberg 150 CD unit. Improvements to the engine include a re-designed four-port cylinder head based on the company's experience with the Triumph Spitfire in racing, which increases the power output, and a water-heated jacket on the inlet manifold which shortens the warming-up period and gives better mixture distribution. There is also a 'no-loss' cooling system which collects the overflow when the engine is warm and returns it into the system when the engine cools down.

The really unique feature of the 1300 is its transmission. The engine, gearbox and final drive are all integrated and flexibly mounted on a rubber-based sub-frame. The power unit is placed longitudinally so that the front-drive power pack does not adversely affect the car's turning circle. This has, in fact, been kept down to 30ft.

The clutch is of the diaphragm type and the whole clutch unit can be replaced without removing the engine or transmission by simply withdrawing the 'quill' shaft which transmits the drive from the clutch to the transfer gear train.

The floor-mounted, centrally-placed gear-shift lever controls the gearbox, of which all four forward gears are fitted with synchromesh.

The oil supplies of engine and transmission are separated.

Rotaflex couplings and Rzeppa-type constant velocity joints are employed in the drive shafts between the hypoid bevel final drive and the front wheels.

Suspension is independent with coil springs all round. At front, use is made of combined spring and shock-absorber units. At rear the suspension is of the semi-

*For 1300 TC see page 66

Fig. 3. Top view, showing forward-opening bonnet

trailing arm type. The brake system incorporates $8\frac{3}{4}$in discs at front and drums at rear, the latter with leading and trailing shoes.

The body and the chassis form a unitary monocoque construction. Steering is by rack and pinion and the steering column is fully adjustable for both rake and height. This adjustment is controlled by a knurled hand-wheel located within easy reach of the driver.

Both front seats are adjustable fore and aft, and in addition the driver's seat is adjustable for rake and height with $1\frac{1}{4}$in total movement. The rear seat has a centre folding armrest. There is an enclosed lockable glove compartment in the facia and a full-width parcel tray beneath. The fully-lined 11 cu ft luggage compartment accommodates the spare wheel recessed in the floor and has a counterbalanced lid.

Both front doors lock externally with the ignition key and the rear doors have childproof safety catches. All interior door handles are flush-fitting. The window winding handles are of the fold-away type.

The facia/instrument panel incorporates a unique 'radar-type' screen on which appears a comprehensive system of eight warning lights to tell the driver all he needs to know about the operation of the car. In different colours and clearly marked, are warning lights for low charge, low oil pressure, low fuel, parking brake

Fig. 4. Interior view, front compartment and facia

on, main beam and direction indicators (see Fig. 5).

There is a large-capacity heater which provides fresh heated or cold air to the windscreen and below the dashboard. An air extraction system causes the air to flow to the rear of the car; it is then channelled through the parcel shelf into the boot, from whence it flows through the hollow rear window pillars and is extracted through valved ventilator slots above the rear window. This process assists in rear window demisting.

IDENTIFICATION

Engine number: The engine number is stamped on the left-hand side of the cylinder block, above the fuel pump.

Commission number: The commission (or car/chassis number) is stamped on the identification plate which is attached to the top of the left-hand front wing valance, adjacent to the front suspension top mounting. This plate also carries the Paint and Trim code numbers.

The commission number is prefixed by the car model series designation (RD) and suffixed by two letters indicating the body style (DL, four-door Saloon).

Serial numbers (approximate and for guidance only):

September 1965	RD	1 DL
January 1966	RD	2025 DL
January 1967	RD20420 DL	

MODIFICATIONS

No modifications of importance have been introduced so far. Early-production cars showed up minor faults resulting in certain modifications in production; where deemed necessary, these are mentioned in the section *Repair Data*.

For the 1968 model year the 1300 was continued unchanged but an additional higher-performance model was introduced (see page 66).

PRICES (UK)

	Basic	*Purchase Tax*	*Total*
January 1966	£658	£138.12.11	£796.12.11
May 1966	£678	£142.16.3	£820.16.3
July 1966	£678	£157.1.10	£835.1.10
October 1967	£678	£157.1.10	£835.1.10

INSTRUMENTS AND CONTROLS

1 Glove compartment
2 Interior light switch
3 Blower motor switch
4 Heater control levers
5 Instrument lights rheostat switch
6 Light switch
7 Choke control
8 Ignition/starter switch
9 Speedometer/distance recorder (trip and total)
10 Warning indicator light cluster, incorporating:
'OIL' (green): oil pressure warning light;
'BEAM' (blue): headlight high beam indicator light;
'IGN' (red): ignition/generator charging indicator light;
'FUEL' (red): operates when fuel in tank is down to or below approx. $1\frac{1}{2}$ Imp gallons;
'H.BRAKE' (yellow): parking brake applied;
'CHOKE' (yellow): operates when choke control is being used.
In addition there are two arrowed direction indicator warning lights (green)

11 Engine cooling system temperature gauge (C–H)
12 Fuel gauge (E–$\frac{1}{2}$–F; tank capacity $11\frac{3}{4}$ Imp gallons)
13 Ammeter (D–C)
14 Windscreen-washer control
15 Windscreen-wiper switch
16 Ashtray
17 Trip mileage recorder resetting control
18 Water valve control (for heater)
19 Lights selector switch, incorporating headlight flasher
20 Horn push
21 Steering column adjustment clamp handwheel
22 Direction-indicator switch
23 Bonnet lock control

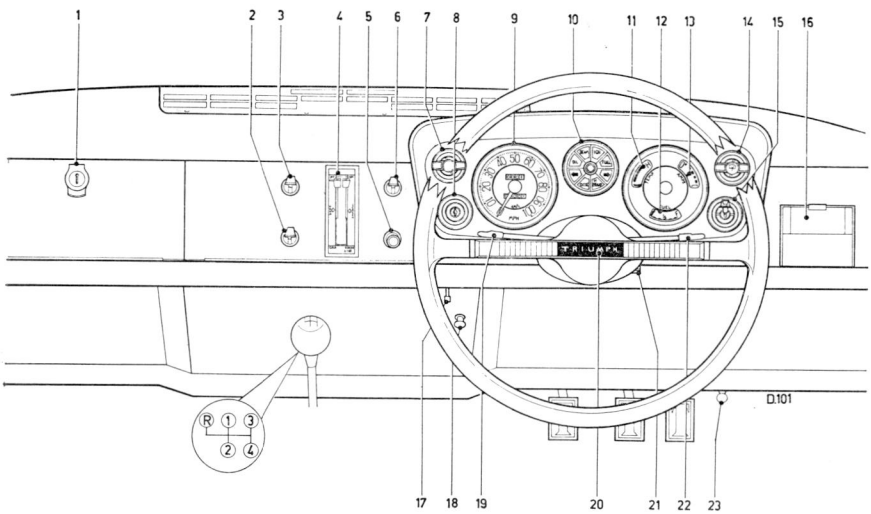

Fig. 5. Instruments and controls

Dimensions and Weights

EXTERIOR DIMENSIONS

	inches
Wheelbase	$96\frac{5}{8}$
Track, front	53*
Track, rear	$52\frac{5}{8}$
Overall length	153
Overall width	$61\frac{3}{4}$
Overall height (unladen)	54
Ground clearance	$5\frac{1}{2}$
Turning circle	360 (30 ft)
Front door gap (at waist)	36
Rear door gap (at waist)	24

*Static laden, nominal.

INTERIOR DIMENSIONS

	inches
Pedal to front seat, maximum	40
Steering wheel to seat	6
Steering wheel to seat backrest, maximum	21
Height over front seat	38
Height of front seat	14
Maximum adjustment of front seat	6
Depth of front seat	20
Width of front seats (each)	22
Front seat backrest to rear seat, maximum	12

Height over rear seat	34
Height of rear seat	12½
Depth of rear seat	18½
Width of rear seat (effective)	45
Maximum interior height	45
Maximum interior width	52
Height of luggage compartment, minimum	13
Height of luggage compartment, maximum	18
Depth of luggage compartment	33
Width of luggage compartment, minimum	40
Width of luggage compartment, maximum	51½
Capacity of luggage compartment	11 cu ft

WEIGHTS

(manufacturer's data, approximate)

Dry weight	17 cwt (1904 lb)
Kerb weight	18 cwt (2016 lb)
Gross vehicle weight, maximum	23¼ cwt (2604 lb)

Technical Specifications*

ENGINE

Type:	four-stroke, petrol, water-cooled
Cylinders:	four, in-line
Valve arrangement:	overhead valves, pushrod-operated
Bore and stroke (inches):	2·9 x 2·99
(mm:	73·7 x 76·0
Cubic capacity (cu in):	79·2
(cc):	1296
Piston area (sq in):	26·5
Compression ratio:	8·5 : 1
Maximum bhp (net) at rpm:	61 at 5000
Maximum bmep at rpm:	139 lb/sq in at 3000
Maximum torque (net) at rpm:	73 lb ft at 3000
Mean piston speed at maximum bhp:	2492 ft/min
Top gear mph at 1000 rpm:	15·40
Top gear mph at 2500 ft/min piston speed:	79
Carburettor:	single Stromberg 150 CD

TRANSMISSION

Clutch:	single dry plate, 6½ in
Gearbox:	4-speed, all synchromesh, and reverse
Gearbox ratios to 1:	1·06, 1·45, 2·16, 3·40, R.3·99
Overall gear ratios to 1:	4·37, 5·96, 8·87, 13·97, R.16·39
Final drive, type:	hypoid, driving front wheels
ratio:	4·11 : 1

*For 1300 TC see page 66

CHASSIS

Chassis construction:	unitary body-cum-chassis
Suspension, front:	independent, double transverse wishbones, coil springs (high-mounted)
Suspension, rear:	independent, semi-trailing arms, coil springs
Shock-absorbers:	telescopic, front and rear
Steering gear:	Alford and Alder, rack and pinion
Steering wheel, number of turns:	$3\frac{1}{4}$ from lock to lock
Wheels:	steel disc, 4-stud
Wheel rim size:	4J x 13
Tyres, type and size:	Dunlop C41 tubeless, 5.60–13
Tyre pressures:	see page 11
Brakes, type:	Girling disc/drum, hydraulic; parking brake operates rear brakes mechanically
Brakes, dimensions:	discs (front) $8\frac{3}{4}$ in diameter drums (rear) 8 in diameter, $1\frac{1}{4}$ in wide
front, lining area:	15·5 sq in
swept area:	145 sq in
rear, lining area:	38 sq in
swept area:	63 sq in
total, lining area:	53·5 sq in
swept area:	208 sq in

ELECTRICAL EQUIPMENT

Electrical system:	12 volts
Battery:	12 volts, 40 Ah
Earthing:	negative
Ignition:	coil

THEORETICAL ROAD SPEEDS

rpm	first gear (mph)	second gear (mph)	third gear (mph)	top gear (mph)	mean piston speed (ft/min)
(a) 1000	4·80	7·55	11·25	15·40	498
(b) 3000	14·40	22·65	33·75	46·20	1495
(c) 5000	24·00	37·75	56·25	77·00	2492

(b)=engine speed at maximum torque.
(c)=engine speed at maximum bhp.

PERFORMANCE FIGURES

NOTE: These figures are approximate and should be considered to be fair averages.

Maximum speed (mph):	85
Cruising speed (mph):	70
Cruising range (miles):	290
Acceleration (sec):	
0–30 mph through gears:	6
0–40 mph through gears:	9
0–50 mph through gears:	13
0–60 mph through gears:	19
0–70 mph through gears:	30

Standing ¼ mile:	22
20–40 in top gear:	12
30–50 in top gear:	12
40–60 in top gear:	14
50–70 in top gear:	19
Fuel consumption (mpg):	25

Lubrication and Maintenance
RUNNING-IN PERIOD

No specific speeds are recommended for the running-in period. However, to avoid overloading the engine, do not use full throttle at low speeds nor when the engine has not yet attained its normal operating temperature. Full power should not be used until at least 500 miles have been covered, and even then it should only be used for short periods at a time. These periods may be extended as the engine becomes more responsive. After 1000 miles running, the engine can be considered to be fully run-in. At this time, or as near to it as possible, the car should be returned to the dealer or distributor who sold it for a 'Free Service'.

GENERAL DATA

Engine:

Sump capacity (drain and refill):	6¼ Imp pints (7·5 US pints)
Oil viscosity, above 30°C (80°F):	SAE 30 or 20W/40 or 20W/50
30°C down to 0°C (32°F):	SAE 20 or 10W/30 or 20W/40 or 20W/50
below 0°C (32°F):	SAE 10W or 10W/30

Oil dipstick: on right-hand side of engine, at the rear.

Oil drain plug: on left-hand side of sump, adjacent to steering rack.

Oil change period: every 6000 miles or at least every six months (or more frequently under less favourable operating conditions).

Change oil after a run when the engine is hot.

Oil filter: Full-flow oil filter. Renew complete unit every 12,000 miles or at every other oil change. Clean and smear the joint faces with oil before screwing in the new unit in order to ensure an oil-tight seal.

Air cleaner: The carburettor air-cleaner housing contains a replaceable paper element which should be cleaned at 6000-mile or six-monthly intervals and renewed every 12,000 miles or yearly. To clean the element use a low-pressure airline or soft brush to clean between the folds.

Carburettor dashpot: Every 6000 miles or six months the damper should be removed and the dashpot topped-up with the seasonal grade of engine oil. Using the damper as a dipstick, the threaded plug must be ¼in above the dashpot when resistance is felt. Apply a few drops of engine oil to the throttle control linkage joints and pivots.

Ignition distributor: Every 6000 miles or six months the distributor should be serviced as follows: smear the cam profile sparingly with clean oil and apply a few drops of thin machine oil to the screw in the centre of the cam, after removing the rotor arm, and to the breaker arm pivot. Clean and adjust the breaker points to 0·015in.

Water pump: Every 12,000 miles or yearly remove the blanking plug (top of pump housing), screw in a grease nipple (⅛in Briggs taper) and lubricate with a grease-gun containing lithium-base multi-purpose grease until grease exudes from the pressure release hole in the side of the housing.

Cooling system:

Capacity (with heater): 6¼ Imp pints (7·5 US pints).

The pressurised 'no-loss' cooling system incorporates a translucent plastic overflow reservoir which collects excess coolant from the radiator as this expands with heat. Depression is created as the system cools, causing the coolant to flow back into the radiator. The coolant level, visible through the translucent reservoir, should be maintained at half full when cold. To drain the cooling system, move the heater control valve under the dashboard to the 'hot' position, remove the radiator filler cap, open the tap in the bottom of the radiator and the tap at the rear right-hand side of the cylinder block. During frosty periods use an anti-freeze solution which meets BS specification 3151 or 3152.

Gearbox:

Oil capacity:	2¼ Imp pints (2·7 US pints)
Oil grade:	GL4, Hypoid
Oil viscosity, above 0°C (32°F):	SAE 90 EP
below 0°C (32°F):	SAE 80 EP
Oil level/filler plug:	on left-hand side of gearbox
Oil level check:	every 12,000 miles or 12 months

Periodic oil changes are not required.

Final drive/differential:

Oil capacity:	1¼ Imp pints (1·5 US pints)
Oil grade and viscosity:	as for gearbox
Oil level/filler plug:	in front cover of final drive housing
Oil level check:	every 12,000 miles or 12 months

Periodic oil changes are not required.

Steering gear: Every 12,000 miles (or yearly) lubricate the steering unit by applying a grease-gun containing lithium-base multi-purpose grease to the nipple provided at the bottom of the steering pinion housing.

Brake and clutch system: Every month and at every 6000-mile service check the fluid level in the brake and clutch master cylinder reservoirs. Clean the caps before removing them. If necessary, top-up the fluid till the level coincides with the level mark on the side of the reservoirs. Use Castrol Girling Crimson Clutch and Brake Fluid, or, if this is not available, another fluid which meets the SAE 70R3 specification.

Jacking: Four-point side jacking with scissor-type jack. To lift the vehicle, raise the jack until it locates in the jacking socket in the underside of the body sill adjacent to the wheel to be lifted.

TYRE PRESSURES

Take pressures when the tyres are cold and if necessary adjust as follows:

Front:	22 lb/sq in
Rear:	22 lb/sq in

ROUTINE MAINTENANCE

NOTE: See also *General Data* on page 10.

Daily: Check engine oil level, fuel tank, tyres.

Weekly: Check battery electrolyte, tyre pressures, cooling system.

Monthly: Check fluid level of brake and clutch fluid reservoirs, top-up if necessary.

A. Every 6000 miles or every 6 months:

*A*1 Engine sump: drain (when hot) and refill.

*A*2 Gearbox: check oil level, top-up if necessary.

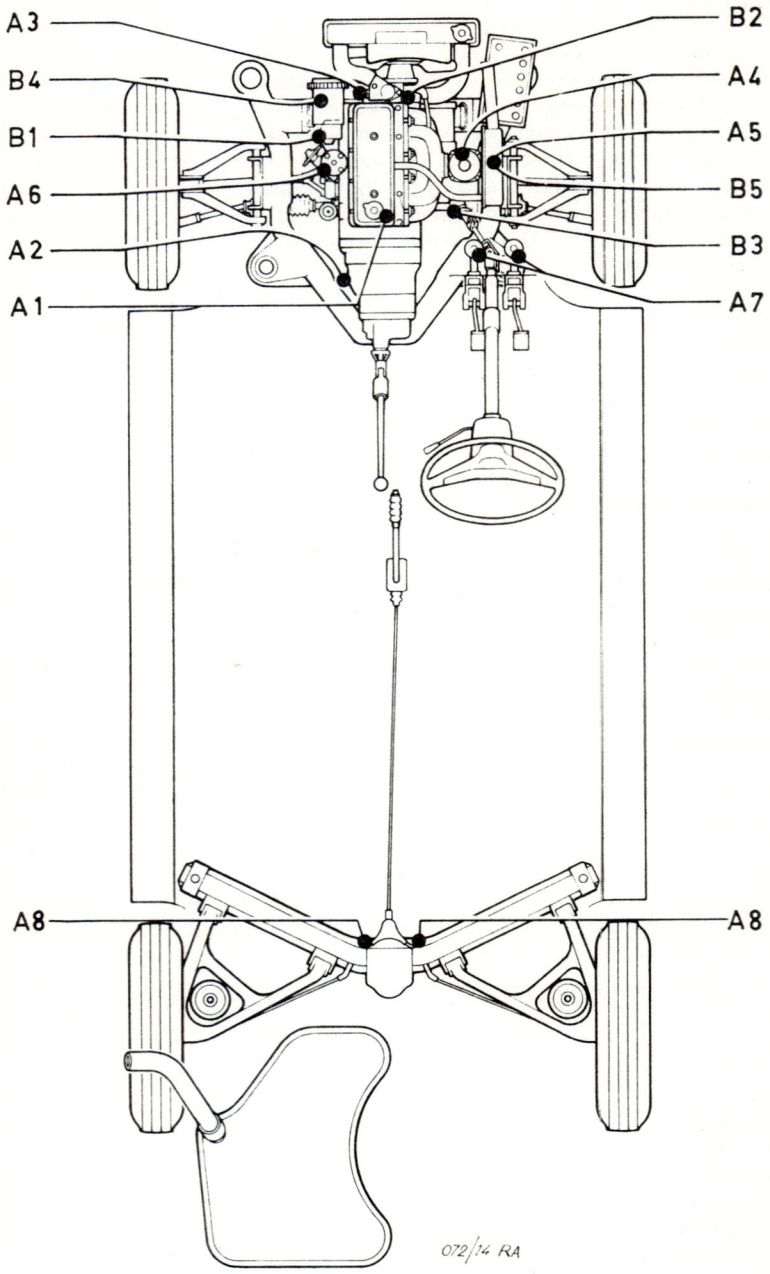

A3
B4
B1
A6
A2
A1

B2
A4
A5
B5
B3
A7

A8   A8

072/14 RA

Fig. 6. Lubrication chart

*A*3 Differential: check oil level, top-up if necessary.
*A*4 Carburettor: top-up dashpot with engine oil.
*A*5 Air cleaner (dry type): clean paper element and filter housing.
*A*6 Ignition distributor: lubricate as outlined on page 10.
*A*7 Brake and clutch fluid reservoirs: check fluid level, top-up if necessary.
*A*8 Parking brake: lubricate cable and linkage with grease.
   Controls: lubricate linkage points of carburettor, accelerator and pedal pivot bushes with engine oil.
   Bodywork: lubricate locks, hinges etc. with engine oil.
   Engine: check fan-belt, valve clearances, engine idling.
   Ignition system: check spark plugs, contact breaker points, ignition timing and advance.
   Clutch: check hydraulic pipes for leaks.
   Steering: check wheel alignment by condition of tyre tread; check constant velocity joint gaiters for damage.
   Brake system: check hydraulic pipes for leaks, chafing and hose clearance; adjust brake shoes.
   Electrical: check all equipment for correct functioning.
   Road wheels: check wheel nuts for tightness.

B. Every 12,000 miles or yearly:
*B*1 Engine oil filter: renew filter unit.
*B*2 Water pump: lubricate with grease-gun (remove plug, fit nipple).
*B*3 Steering unit: lubricate with grease-gun (1 nipple, 5 strokes only).
*B*4 Dynamo: lubricate rear bearing with a few drops of engine oil.
*B*5 Air cleaner (dry type): renew paper element.
   Fuel system: clean out fuel pump; renew cork gasket if necessary.
   Ignition system: renew spark plugs.
   Exhaust system: check for leaks and/or damage.
   Transmission: check drive-shaft coupling bolts.
   Steering: check connections and mounting bolts.
   Brake system: examine brake pads, linings and wheel cylinders; clean brake drums and linings.

C. Every 36,000 miles:
Brake system: renew rubber seals in master cylinder and wheel cylinders.

Spring service:
Engine: check cylinder compression pressures; decarbonize and grind-in valves if necessary; tune engine.
Cooling system: change to low temperature thermostat if required; check hose connections for tightness; check fresh-air control for correct functioning.
Brake system: check and if necessary renew brake linings and pads.
Wheels and tyres: re-balance; check tyres for wear.
Body/chassis: wash body and underframe to remove deposits of corrosive salt.

Autumn service:
As for spring service, and in addition:
Ignition system: check spark plugs, contact breaker points and coil intensity.
Cooling system: drain, flush out and refill with anti-freeze mixture; change to high-temperature type thermostat if required; check system and heater controls for correct functioning.
Electrical: check all equipment for correct functioning; check headlamp beam settings; check battery condition.

Repair Data

Repairs are best performed by authorised Triumph dealers, who possess special tools and the necessary experience. These data have been compiled from the official repair manuals, and other technical publications, supplied through the kind co-operation of Standard-Triumph International Ltd., Coventry, England.

ENGINE*

Description:

Water-cooled, four-cylinder, four-stroke ohv petrol engine, in unit with clutch, gearbox and final drive, mounted on a sub-frame separate from the main body of the car on two rubber mountings. The engine can be removed and installed, leaving the transmission unit in place.

Engine cooling is by a radiator ahead of the engine, forming the main part of the 'no-loss' pressurised cooling system. This system employs a separate coolant reservoir which collects overflow when the engine is hot; this residual coolant, which would be lost in conventional cooling systems, is here returned into the

*For 1300 TC see page 66

Fig. 7. Engine, under-bonnet view

Fig. 8. Engine/transmission unit, side view

system when the engine has cooled down sufficiently. Circulation of the coolant is assisted by an impeller-type water pump and the water pump pulley is fitted with a four-bladed fan. A thermostat, fitted between the water pump and the water outlet pipe situated at the front of the cylinder head, serves to assist quick engine warm-up and maintain correct operating temperature.

The system is fitted with two drain cocks—one located in the bottom of the radiator, the other at the rear right-hand side of the cylinder block. The water pump is driven in tandem with the generator by means of a V-belt from the crankshaft pulley; the belt can be adjusted in the conventional manner by pivoting the generator away from or toward the engine as necessary.

The cast-iron cylinder head incorporates the overhead valve mechanism and is mounted on the cylinder block by means of studs and nuts. The separate inlet and exhaust manifolds are situated on the right-hand side of the engine. No 'hot-spot' valve is fitted. The inlet manifold is heated by means of an incorporated water jacket through which the coolant is forced by the action of the water pump. The valves, which are positioned vertically and in-line, are fitted to replaceable valve guides. The valve seats are integral in the cylinder head and can eventually be replaced, if necessary, with steel inserts. The valves are secured by means of valve spring retainers of the 'key-hole' type, no separate split valve keepers being fitted. Both inlet and exhaust valves are fitted with single valve springs. The valves are operated by steel rockers, offset in pairs and mounted on a hollow steel rocker shaft resting in four supports on the cylinder head. The distance between the rockers,

Fig. 9. Engine/transmission unit and front suspension, front view

Fig. 10. Engine/transmission unit and front suspension, rear view

with the exception of the two outside pairs, is maintained by means of steel spacer springs. Solid steel pushrods, operated by hollow steel valve tappets, transmit camshaft action to the valve train.

The cast-steel camshaft runs in four bearings, machined directly into the left-hand side of the cylinder block. Camshaft end-float is taken by a semi-circular thrust plate located in a groove in the front of the camshaft; this plate is held in place by two locating bolts. The camshaft is crankshaft driven by means of a single roller timing chain and sprockets. This chain is tensioned by a non-adjustable spring-blade type chain tensioner, attached to the inside of the timing chain cover. Adjacent to the intermediate camshaft bearing journal, the camshaft carries a skew gear which drives the ignition distributor and the Hobourn-Eaton eccentric rotor-type oil pump.

The cast-iron crankshaft runs in three main bearings which consist of replaceable steel-backed bearing shells, lined with bearing material. These main bearing shells are available in standard and four undersizes. Crankshaft end-float is taken at the rear main bearing by means of semi-circular thrust washers. All main bearing caps are numbered for identification purposes and match the corresponding numbers stamped on the crankcase housing. The crankshaft, flywheel and clutch assembly are dynamically balanced as a unit. The cast-iron starter wheel with shrunk-on starter ring gear is externally secured to the crankshaft flange by means of four bolts and a dowel.

The aluminium pistons are of split-skirt type. Each is fitted with two compression rings and one oil control ring, all fitted above the hollow steel piston pin, which is an interference fit in the small-end of the connecting rod. The connecting rods are steel forgings of I-beam section. The big-end bearings are replaceable steel-backed bearing shells lined with bearing material.

The cast-iron cylinder block, incorporating the upper crankcase, has integral cylinder bores. If the cylinder bores are worn or damaged, they can be bored-out to suit the nearest oversize piston; if, however, the bores are worn beyond re-bore limits, new cast-iron dry cylinder liners can be pressed in, after which new standard-size pistons can be installed.

The engine sump is formed by a separate compartment in the top of the transmission/final drive casing to which the engine is bolted. The sealed crankcase breathing system incorporates a pipe connecting the rocker cover to the carburettor air filter which enables the fumes to be drawn from the crankcase and fed to the carburettor intake.

An externally-mounted full-flow oil filter of the 'throw-away' type is screwed on to the left-hand side of the crankcase. During a cold start in winter, or if the oil-filter element becomes contaminated and eventually clogged, the pressure build-up opens a relief valve in the oil-filter housing, allowing the oil to by-pass the filter and flow directly into the main oil gallery, thus lubricating the engine with unfiltered oil. The oil enters the oil pump through a wire mesh screen and is then pumped to the oil filter. When a pressure of 45–55 lb/sq in is exceeded, a spring-loaded relief valve, located between the oil pump and the filter unit, opens, allowing surplus oil to return to the sump. After the oil has passed through the filter element, it is forced into the main oil gallery; this is a longitudinal drilling in the left-hand side of the cylinder block.

From the main oil gallery, the oil is distributed via cross-drillings in the cylinder block to the camshaft and crankshaft bearings, and through drillings in the crankshaft webs to the connecting-rod bearings. The cylinder bores and piston pins are lubricated by oil escaping from the crankshaft bearings. From the rearmost camshaft bearing the oil is metered upward through a vertical drilling in the cylinder block and another drilling in the cylinder head, into the drilled rearmost rockershaft support and then to the hollow rocker shaft. The rocker shaft has crossdrillings where the valve rockers are fitted, thus lubricating all moving parts of the valve rocker mechanism before returning to the sump.

The single side-draught Stromberg 150 CD carburettor receives petrol from the rear-mounted fuel tank by means of an AC mechanically-operated fuel pump of diaphragm-type, driven by an eccentric on the camshaft and located on the left-hand side of the crankcase. The air cleaner consists of a pressed steel housing containing a replaceable paper element, which should be cleaned and subsequently replaced at regular intervals.

The ignition system is of the conventional battery and coil variety, employing a Lucas distributor with centrifugal and vacuum advance control.

Removal and installation of the engine/transmission unit:

Removal:

(1) In the driving compartment: remove the parcel shelf, gear-lever knob, transmission covers carpet and panel, and gear lever; detach the speedometer cable from transmission; the clutch fluid pipe from the clutch operating cylinder. Remove the rear mounting and damper assembly from the sub-frame.

Remove the bonnet, marking the hinges to facilitate refitting.

(2) Under the bonnet: drain oil and water, remove the radiator hoses and radiator assembly; remove the battery.

(3) Disconnect the starter cable, engine earth lead, temperature transmitter, ignition coil and generator and oil pressure switch wires; move the wiring harness clear of the engine.

(4) Disconnect and remove the heater blower motor, the heater pipes and control valve from the manifold, and the water pipe.

(5) Disconnect the carburettor controls, the petrol inlet pipe from fuel pump and the exhaust pipe from the manifold.

(6) Compress the Rotoflex couplings using tool No. S.328 and detach the outer drive shafts from the couplings. Detach the engine mountings from the crossmember and attach a sling to the engine lifting eyes; hoist the unit out of the car.

To remove the engine unit only, leaving the transmission unit in place:

Carry out operations (1) to (5) inclusive and, in addition, remove clutch drive shaft end-plate and drive shaft; remove dipstick and the sump bolts (NOTE: Engine has to be raised 2 in to release front two bolts). Take weight up on a hoist and release front mountings. Lift the engine until the oil-pump intake pipe is clear of the transmission case before manoeuvring the unit clear of the vehicle.

Installation: Installation is a reversal of the removing procedure; be sure to fill the sump and the cooling system.

Dismantling and assembly of the engine:

Dismantling: After the engine has been separated from the transmission unit, dismantling is carried out as follows:

First remove auxiliary equipment such as generator, starter motor, oil-filter unit, water pump, fan, spark plugs and coil. Remove the carburettor, fuel pump and distributor. Remove the oil-pressure switch and oil-pressure relief valve assembly. Remove both manifolds from the cylinder head. Mark the clutch cover and the flywheel. Unscrew the six clutch cover bolts one turn at a time, until the clutch diaphragm spring pressure is relieved; remove the bolts and the clutch assembly.

Remove the valve-rocker cover with its gasket and gradually loosen the rocker-shaft support nuts; lift off the rocker-shaft assembly; withdraw the pushrods and the tappets, keeping them in order of removal to ensure re-installation in their original positions.

The rocker-shaft assembly is dismantled as follows: Take off the split-pins from the rocker-shaft end-caps and slide all the pairs of off-set rockers, thrust washers, rocker-shaft supports and springs from the rocker shaft, keeping them in the order in which they are removed. Remove the locating bolt and its shake-proof washer and remove the rearmost rocker-shaft support.

Gradually loosen all the cylinder-head nuts in reverse order of the recommended tightening sequence (see page 23) and lift the head from the block. Remove and discard the cylinder-head gasket.

The valve assemblies are dismantled by using a suitably shaped piece of wood placed under the valve head for support and, whilst pushing the spring retainer down, move it sideways to allow its larger diameter to move up the valve stem. Keep the released valves, springs and spring retainers in the order of removal to ensure correct re-installation.

Fig. 11. Engine/transmission unit, partly cut-away view

Unscrew the crankshaft hub nut and withdraw the starter wheel and ring gear assembly from the crankshaft. Before removing the crankshaft pulley, note the position of the ignition timing mark on the ring gear carrier in relation to the keyway in the pulley.

Remove the timing cover bolts, gaskets and concave oil-thrower from the crankshaft. If necessary, remove the oil-seal from the timing cover. Bend back the tabs of the camshaft sprocket securing bolts, remove the bolts and simultaneously lever the timing sprockets, together with the timing chain, from their respective shafts. Extract the Woodruff key and remove the shims from the crankshaft.

Release the front engine bearer plate. Remove the semi-circular camshaft thrust flange, withdraw the camshaft, being careful not to damage the bearing bores in the cylinder block. Lift off the engine bearer plate with its gasket. Remove the four flywheel bolts; withdraw the flywheel. Remove the rear engine bearer plate and the crankshaft rear sealing cover. Remove the front sealing block.

Measure the crankshaft end-float and note any necessary correction.

Remove the oil-pump assembly. Remove the main and big-end bearing caps and shells. Be sure to keep the shell bearings with their respective caps. Carefully lift out the crankshaft and remove the remaining upper half main shell bearings, the thrust washers and connecting-rod shell bearings. All caps and bearings should be kept in the order of removal to ensure correct installation. Push the pistons out through the top of the cylinder bores. Remove studs, core seals and other miscellaneous items as necessary.

NOTE: Thoroughly clean and inspect all parts, replacing those that are worn or damaged. Renew all oil-seals, gaskets and locking plates. Make sure all jointing faces are perfectly clean and free from burrs, etc.; check the condition of studs, stud nuts, bolts, lock washers and core seals. Unless the pistons or connecting rods are to be renewed, it is not advisable to remove the piston pins, as they are shrink-fitted in the connecting rods. If necessary, remove the piston pins with tool S.334 or similar suitable special equipment.

If the engine is to be left stripped down for any length of time, coat all moving parts with clean engine oil to prevent rust and corrosion.

Assembly: NOTE: Always renew all gaskets and seals using suitable jointing compound where necessary, and liberally lubricate the moving parts with clean engine oil as work proceeds.

Assemble the overhead valve mechanism by inserting the valves into their respective valve guides. Install the valve springs, noting that the close coiled ends of the springs should be facing the cylinder head. Place the valve retaining washers over the springs and, locating the offset holes of the retainers over the valve stems, press down the retainers, move the retainers sideways to centralise them and release the pressure. If the pistons were removed from the connecting rods, make certain to fit each piston to the same connecting rod from which it was removed. It is also extremely important that the connecting rod is fitted to the piston in the correct position. Each piston has an arrow cast in its crown close to the edge; the arrows on the piston crowns must be nearest to the front of the engine and the connecting-rod big-end bearing caps must be at the left-hand side. To refit the piston pins will require a minimum pressure of $\frac{1}{2}$ ton to force the pin into the bore. To achieve the interference fit use tool S.334 or other suitable special equipment.

Fit the crankshaft main bearing upper shells to the half-bore in the cylinder block from which they were removed (unless new bearing shells are installed). Carefully fit the crankshaft into the cylinder block, taking care not to dislodge the upper main bearing shells. Placing the white metal face of each semi-circular thrust washer against the crankshaft thrust faces, fit them at each side of the rear main bearing in the cylinder block recess. Position the lower main bearing shells in the main bearing caps from which they were removed (unless new bearing shells are installed); install the main bearing caps. Install the main bearing cap bolts and tighten these to 55–60 lb ft. Check that the crankshaft rotates freely and measure crankshaft end-float with the aid of a dial indicator mounted on the front of the crankcase, its index touching the crankcase-end; a feeler gauge can also be used. If the end-float needs correction, one or two oversize thrust washers can be fitted as required. These are available in standard size and one oversize.

Position the piston rings so that their gaps are staggered; the chrome compression ring should be at the top, the taper faced compression ring should be fitted with the taper towards the piston crown. Fit the piston assemblies in their respective cylinder bores (arrows towards the front), using a suitable piston ring compressing tool. Fit the connecting-rod bearing shells to the connecting rods from which they were removed (unless new bearing shells are installed).

Make sure that the locating tabs on the shells are properly seated in the corresponding recesses of the connecting rods, and push the pistons down their cylinder bores until the connecting rods are seated on the crankpin journals. Fit connecting-rod lower shell bearings to their respective bearing caps and fit the bearing caps to their respective connecting rods; ensure that the markings on the bearing caps correspond with those on the connecting rods and that the dowels are properly located. Install new bolts and tighten to 38–42 lb ft. Check that the crankshaft rotates freely.

Coat the ends of the sealing block with jointing compound and locate it in the cylinder block. Use a straight-edge to align the sealing block with the front face of the crankcase; securely tighten both screws. Coat the wooden sealing wedges with jointing compound and drive them into the slots formed between the sealing block and the crankcase. Trim the surplus wood flush with the machined lower flange of the crankcase.

Install the engine front-mounting plate, using a new gasket. The stud, which passes through the top centre hole of the plate, communicates with the water jacket. If this stud has been removed, coat the thread with jointing compound and screw it tightly home to prevent water seepage.

Carefully insert the camshaft into the cylinder block. Install the semi-circular camshaft retaining plate and secure it with the bolts. Locate the rear oil-seal, with its housing, using a new gasket and jointing compound, on to the rear face of the cylinder block, being careful not to damage the sealing lip; if a new seal is fitted, its lip must be facing the cylinder block. Centralise the oil-seal before finally tightening the securing bolts.

Attach the engine rear mounting plate, ensuring that the three replaceable fixing points for the flywheel housing are in good condition.

Install the flywheel, ensuring that the dowel and dowel hole correspond. Tighten the flywheel bolts to 42–46 lb ft.

Fit the oil pump in the crankcase, attach the end-plate and secure the assembly with the three bolts. Install the crankshaft timing sprocket with the same adjustment shims as when dismantled, and install the camshaft sprocket. Push the crankshaft as well as the camshaft as far as possible into the crankcase and check the alignment of both sprockets, using a straight-edge. If the alignment needs adjustment, the required number of shims must be removed or added behind the crankshaft

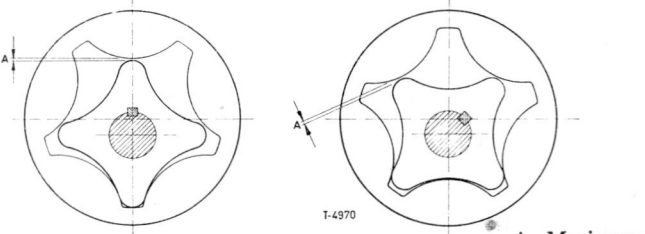

A   Maximum 0·010in.

Fig. 12. Oil pump, rotor clearances

sprocket. When the alignment has been established, remove the sprockets and insert the Woodruff key in the crankshaft.

Rotate the crankshaft until its key-way is exactly at TDC. Hang the timing chain over the sprockets and offer up the sprockets and chain assembly to the two shafts. When installed, the groove marking on the camshaft flange, visible through the unused attaching bolt hole, should 'coincide with the punch marking on the sprocket, adjacent to the aforementioned bolt hole. When correctly installed the scribe lines on both sprockets will be facing each other, whilst coinciding with the centre line passing through both sprockets.

An unmarked camshaft sprocket must be installed after the cylinder head and valve mechanism are fitted. Proceed as follows:

Temporarily fit the camshaft sprocket. Turn the camshaft until valve No. 1 is fully open, then adjust valve No. 8 to 0·040in clearance. Turn the camshaft until valve No. 2 is fully open and adjust valve No. 7 also to 0·040in clearance. Now turn the camshaft until valves Nos. 7 and 8 are just 'balancing' and the clearances of both are equal.

If necessary, turn the crankshaft to bring pistons 1 and 4 to TDC. Carefully remove the camshaft sprocket without disturbing the shaft.

Install the timing chain on both sprockets and offer up the camshaft sprocket to the camshaft. The camshaft sprocket has four equally spaced bolt holes which are offset from the sprocket tooth centre. This provides four different sprocket settings. Half-tooth setting is obtained by rotating the sprocket 90° from its original position. A quarter-tooth adjustment may be obtained by turning the sprocket back to front; when it is turned through 90° from this position, threequarters of a tooth adjustment is obtained.

When the correct sprocket setting has been found, fit the locking plate and the two bolts; tighten the bolts and bend over the locking plate.

Fit the oil thrower to the crankshaft, concave side outwards and, using a hooked tool to compress the chain tensioner to enable it to pass over the chain, fit the timing chain cover, centralising the seal before tightening the screws.

Refit the starter wheel and ring gear assembly. If replacement of the ring gear is necessary, ensure that the starter wheel flange is clean and free from burrs. The ring gear must be fitted with the chamfer on the teeth facing forwards (see also page 24). Fit the crankshaft pulley, engaging the pulley keyway so that it is in the same relative position to the ring gear as was noted prior to dismantling the engine.

Insert the oil pump drive shaft into the distributor mounting bore, making sure the drive tongue on the lower end of the shaft engages properly with the drive slot in the oil pump rotor. Measure the thickness of a plain washer; fit the washer and the distributor drive gear over the shaft, and install the distributor mounting pedestal. Measure the gap between the pedestal and the cylinder block with feeler gauges. Subtract this dimension from the thickness of the washer in order to determine the end-float of the gear. The end-float should be 0·003 to 0·007in; this can be obtained by fitting the requisite number of paper gaskets beneath the pedestal.

Rotate the crankshaft until piston No. 1 is exactly at TDC and at the end of its compression stroke. Lower the driving gear into the bush, allowing it to rotate as it meshes with the camshaft gear and oil pump driving dog. When the drive gear is resting on its bush, the off-set distributor drive slots on top of the gear should be in the 'two and eight o'clock' positions, with the larger segment towards the outside.

Fit the pedestal with the requisite number of paper gaskets and secure with the two spring washers and nuts.

Install the valve tappets in the bores from which they were removed. New tappets are a selective fit and they should slide down their bore by their own weight when lightly oiled.

Fit a new cylinder-head gasket, coated on both sides with jointing compound, over the cylinder-head attaching studs, and carefully lower the cylinder head into position. Install the plain washers and the nuts, and tighten all nuts progressively to the requisite torque of 42–46lb ft, in the following sequence:

	9	3	1	6	8
Front					
	7	5	2	4	10

Install the valve pushrods in their respective places, making sure that their spherical ends are properly seated in the valve tappets. Install the valve rocker-shaft assembly, tightening down the stud-nuts evenly to a torque of 28–30lb ft. Adjust the valve clearance, preferably before installing the spark plugs, to facilitate rotating the crankshaft.

Fit a new engine-to-sump gasket, carefully lower the engine onto the transmission casing and bolt the two assemblies together. Fit the clutch unit to the flywheel using the input shaft to centralise the driven plate. Refit the input shaft using a new circlip, and also the end-plate. Refit the 'O' rings and the two long bolts beneath the transmission casing.

When the unit is installed in the vehicle, the ancillary engine equipment can be fitted. This is a reversal of the dismantling procedure.

Do not forget to fill the sump with the recommended engine oil and the cooling system with water.

Details of reconditioning and servicing of engine components:

Cylinder head: Do not remove the cylinder head unless it is completely cold; if this is not observed, the cylinder head may become warped.

The valve stem to valve guide clearance should be checked by inserting a new valve, lifting it $\frac{1}{8}$in from its seat and rocking it sideways. The movement of the valve head in relation to the valve seat should not be in excess of 0·020in. If necessary, install a new valve guide, using Churchill tool No. S.60A-6.

The top of the newly-fitted valve guide should protrude 0·749 to 0·751in above the top of the cylinder head. The valve guide should be pulled into the cylinder head from the valve spring side with its chamfered edge leading. Use of the correct limiting sleeves will ensure the correct protrusion of the valve guide above the cylinder head.

When the original valve seats cannot be rectified by recutting, the seats should be bored out. If the inlet as well as the exhaust valve seat of one cylinder are to be replaced, first bore out the inlet seat, fit the inlet seat insert, and then bore out the exhaust valve seat recess, cutting it in the edge of the inlet valve seat insert. After recutting or replacing the valve seats, reface the valves, after which they should be lapped-in, using a suitable valve grinding compound.

If the valve head thickness measured at the face edge is less than 1/32in, a new valve should be installed. Before fitting the valves, be sure all grinding swarf is removed; lubricate the valve guides prior to installation.

Pistons: When fitting new pistons to cylinder bores, ensure that they are both of the same grade marking. Pistons are available in standard and two oversizes, the standard size being sub-divided into two grading dimensions, indicated by the symbols 'F', 'G'. These grade markings are always stamped on the tops of new standard-size pistons as well as on the cylinder block, adjacent to the cylinder bores. The piston diameter is measured across the thrust face, at the top and at the bottom of the skirt.

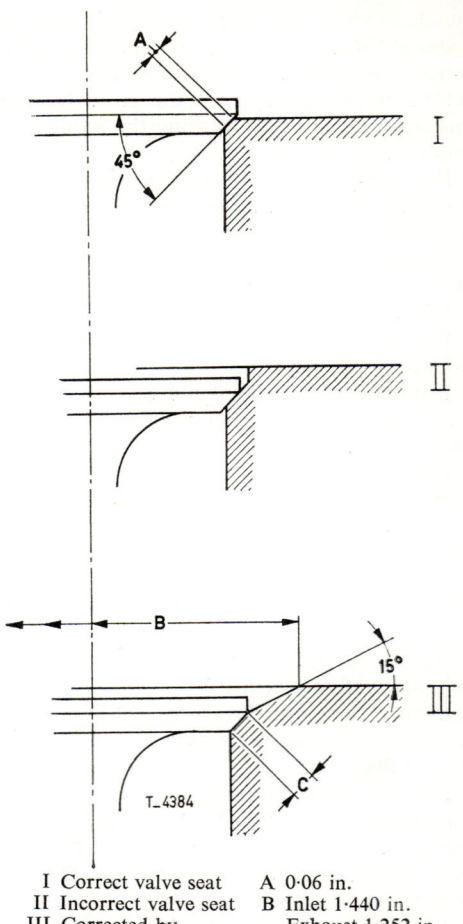

I Correct valve seat	A 0·06 in.
II Incorrect valve seat	B Inlet 1·440 in.
III Corrected by	Exhaust 1·252 in.
cutting to 15° angle	C Maximum 0·10 in.

Fig. 13. Valve seat re-conditioning

Cylinders: Measure the cylinder bore diameters with a cylinder gauge or a dial indicator; insert the gauge into the cylinder bore and take readings at several points in order to determine the maximum bore wear. If the cylinders are worn beyond the permissible tolerance (see *Technical Data*), they should be re-bored to suit the nearest oversize piston size. If cylinders are worn beyond re-bore limits, install new dry liners and standard-size pistons.

Flywheel: If the flywheel clutch face is damaged or scored, it can be re-machined on a lathe; do not exceed the tolerances given in *Technical Data*. A badly damaged or scored flywheel should be replaced.

Starter ring gear: If the starter ring gear needs replacing it is advisable to renew the complete starter wheel assembly as this is a dynamically balanced unit.

 1 Rotor
 2 Insulating bush
 3 Breaker arm and insulating washer
 4 Condenser (capacitor)
 5 Insulating washer
 6 Adjustable breaker point
 7, 8 Base-plate assembly
 9 Breaker cam
10 Spring, centrifugal advance
11 Weight, centrifugal advance
12 Distributor shaft with mounting plate for
   centrifugal advance mechanism
13 Thrust washer
14 Connector and insulating block
15 Vacuum advance diaphragm unit
16 Knurled nut with spring and circlip
17 Distributor housing
18 Seal ring

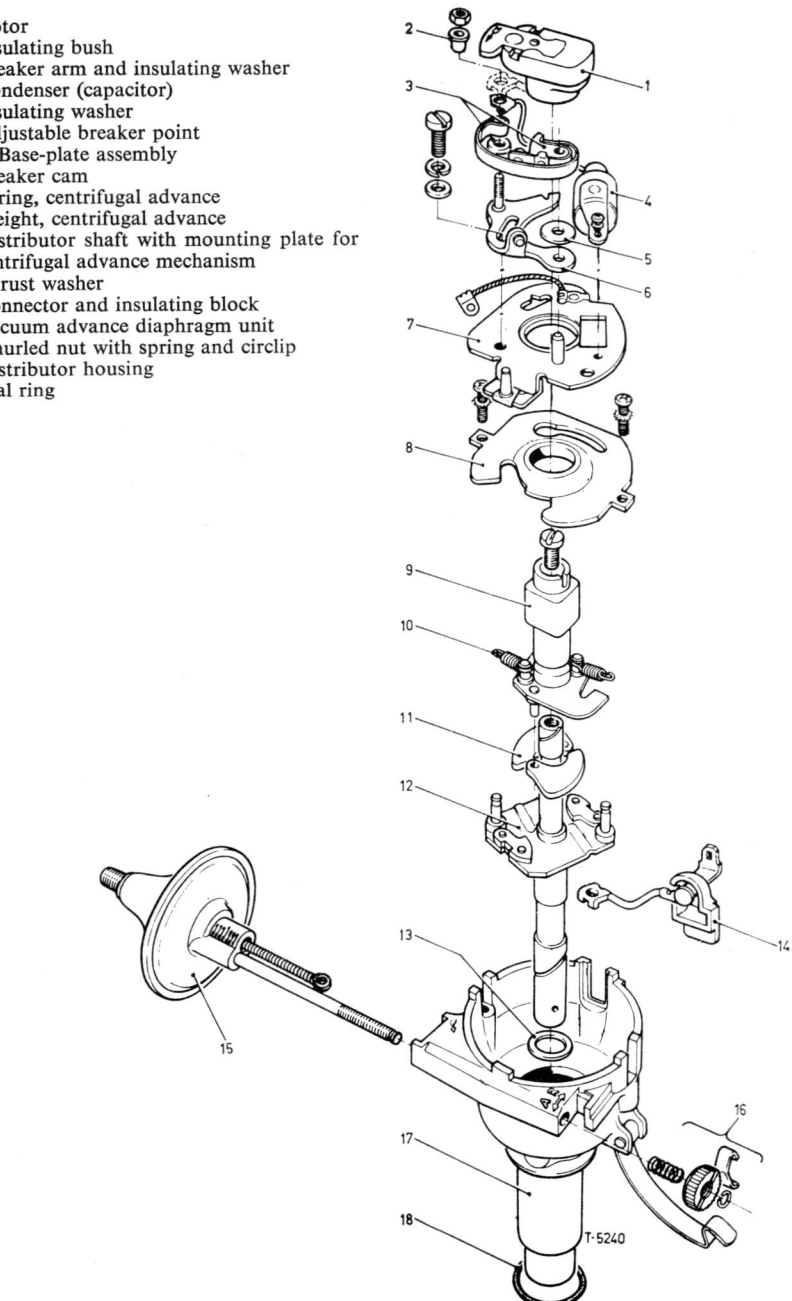

Fig. 14. Ignition distributor, exploded view

1 Pulley
2 Snap ring
3 Ball-bearing
4 Spacer bush
5 Ball-bearing
6 Bearing seal
7 Woodruff key
8 Water-pump shaft
9 Bearing housing
10 Water seal
11 Impeller
12 Water-pump housing
13 Thermostat
14 Thermostat cover
15 Temperature gauge transmitter
16 Gasket

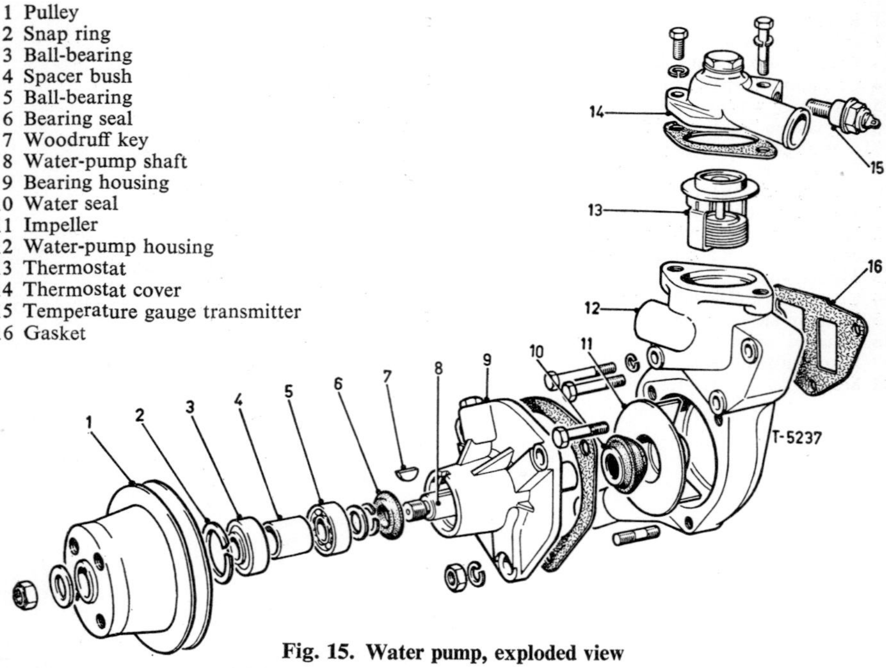

Fig. 15. Water pump, exploded view

Ignition distributor timing: Adjust the contact points to 0·015in. Secure the distributor clamp-plate to the mounting pedestal and lower the distributor into its bore, ensuring that the driving dog properly engages with the drive slot of the gear. Rotate the crankshaft until piston No. 1 is on its compression stroke. Very slowly continue turning the crankshaft until the mark in the starter ring window is in line with the leading edge of the fixed pointer on the timing chain cover; the piston is now at 10° BTDC. The distributor rotor arm should now be pointing towards the No. 1 spark plug lead segment inside the distributor cap. Connect a 12-volt lamp between the primary terminal on the distributor housing and earth, and turn on the ignition switch. Keep the rotor turned clockwise as far as it will go to take up all slack in the drive; if necessary, turn the distributor housing anti-clockwise until the lamp is out. Now slowly turn the housing clockwise until the breaker points just start to open, at which time the lamp will go on. Then tighten the distributor clamp bolt. If necessary, the adjustment may be corrected during a road test, by turning the knurled nut on the vernier control towards R or A in order to retard or advance the ignition respectively.

Water pump: After removal, the water pump may be dismantled as follows:

Detach the bearing housing from the pump body and remove the pulley. Then, using a press and suitable adaptors, extract the impeller and seal from the pump shaft. Remove the bearing retaining circlip from the housing bore and drift out the shaft, complete with its bearings.

From the pump shaft, remove the following parts: key, bearings, spacer bush, circlip, washer and seal ring. Complete dismantling by removing the sealing gland from the recess in the impeller.

Inspect the gland face in the bearing housing for score marks and if necessary

1 Cover
2 Gasket
3 Screen
4 Pump body, upper half
5 Valve gasket
6 Pump inlet and outlet valves
7 Valve clamping plate
8 Pump diaphragm
9 Diaphragm spring
10 Washer
11 Seal ring
12 Pump body, lower half
13 Priming lever assembly
14 Retainer
15 Pump arm shaft
16 Washer
17 Pump lever
18 Return spring
19 Operating fork

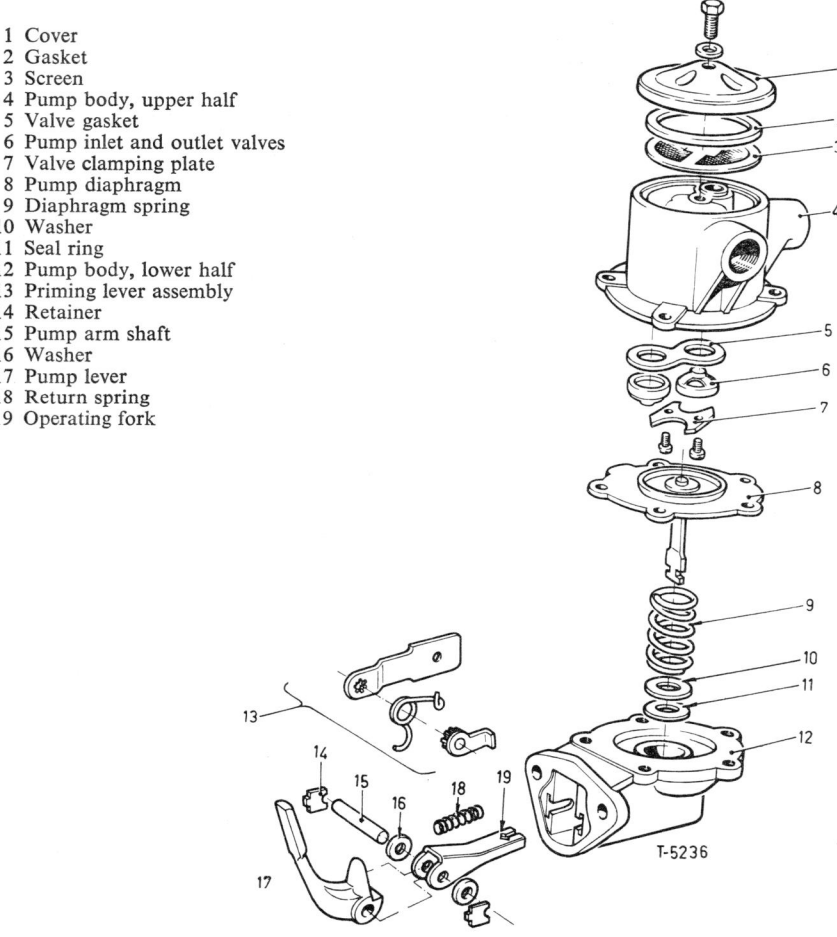

Fig. 16. Fuel pump, exploded view

use Churchill tool No. S.126 to recondition the face.

The distance between the gland face and the mounting face of the pump housing must not exceed 0·265 in.

Reassembly is a direct reversal of the dismantling procedure. When pressing the impeller on to the shaft, ensure that the clearance between the impeller face and the rear face of the housing is 0·030 in. Solder the impeller to the shaft to prevent water leakage between the impeller bore and the shaft. Smear both sides of a new gasket with grease, and secure the assembled bearing housing to the pump body.

Fuel pump: The AC mechanical fuel pump is of the diaphragm type. Before dismantling the pump, mark both flanges to facilitate reassembly. Dismantle from the top, working downwards (see Fig. 16), ensuring that the diaphragm is turned 90° anti-clockwise before lifting it out.

Carburettor: The Zenith-Stromberg carburettor, model 150 CD, operates on the 'constant vacuum' principle, the choke area and the jet orifice varying according

C

1 Damper valve assembly
2 Diaphragm cover/suction chamber
3 Diaphragm spring (later models)
4 Spring seat/diaphragm plate
5 Diaphragm
6 Air valve
7 Jet needle
8 Carburettor body
9 Needle clamping screw
10 Lift pin
11 Throttle lever assembly
12 Starter bar
13 Throttle valve and spindle assembly
14 Choke cam assembly
15 Float needle valve and seal

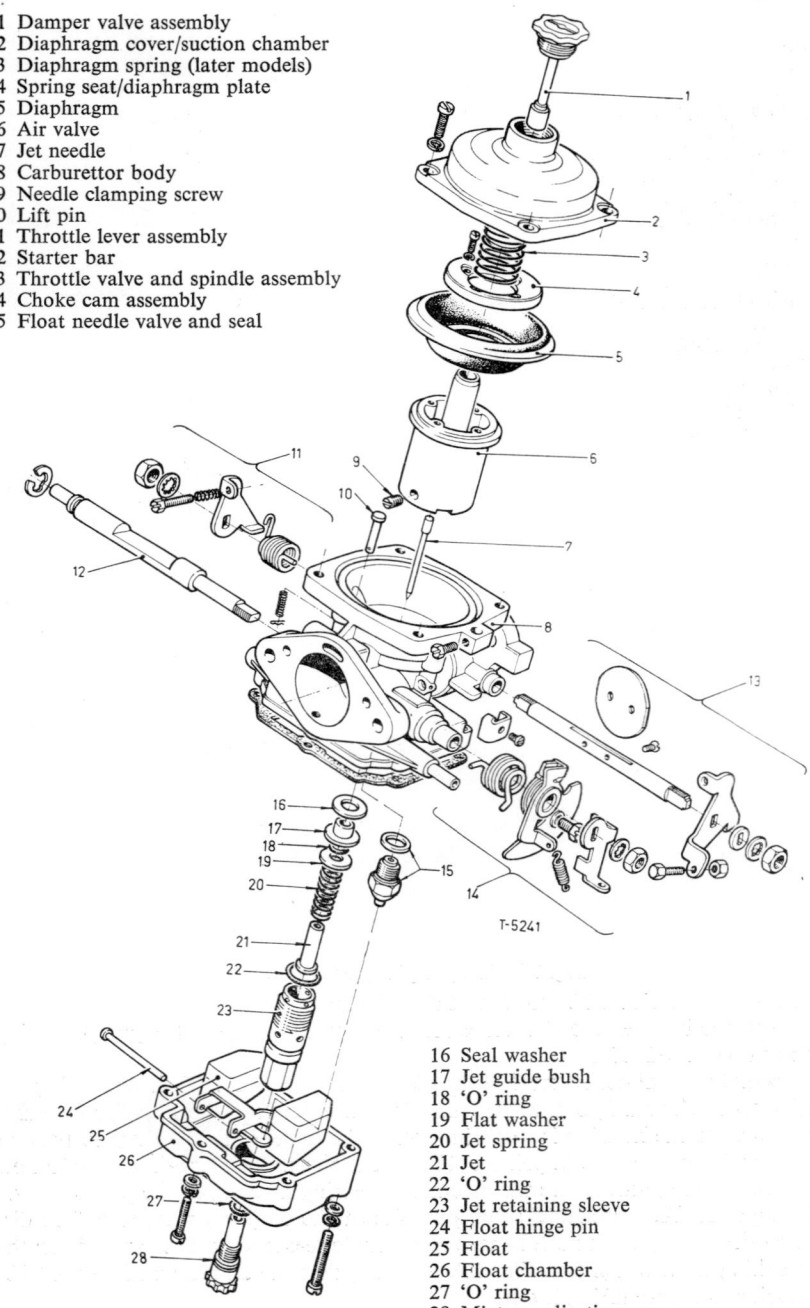

T-5241

16 Seal washer
17 Jet guide bush
18 'O' ring
19 Flat washer
20 Jet spring
21 Jet
22 'O' ring
23 Jet retaining sleeve
24 Float hinge pin
25 Float
26 Float chamber
27 'O' ring
28 Mixture adjusting screw

Fig. 17. Stromberg 150 CD carburettor, exploded view, typical

to the degree of throttle opening and the speed of the engine, which will alter according to the load. It is provided with a concentric float chamber.

Three die-cast aluminium main castings are used in the construction: the main body, suction chamber cover and the float chamber.

The carburettor is provided with a manually controlled cold-start device, interconnected with the throttle to provide for a specific degree of throttle opening to ensure a suitable fast idle while the engine is cold.

Principle of operation: The fuel enters the float chamber through a pipe connection at the side of the main body and via a needle valve, which is actuated by means of a twin rubber float. The fuel from the float chamber will rise in the jet through drillings in the jet assembly, the fuel in the jet orifice being maintained at the same level as that in the float chamber.

Starting from cold: The choke control knob on the instrument panel operates a lever at the side of the carburettor; this lever rotates the starter bar, which lifts the air valve wherein is fitted the metering needle. This movement of the needle increases the area of the annulus between needle and orifice, in this manner enriching the mixture to facilitate cold starting.

At the same time the cam of the lever will open the throttle beyond the normal idle position to a setting determined by the fast-idle screw. When the engine fires, the increased depression will lift the air valve to weaken the initial starting mixture and prevent the engine from stalling through over-richness. The car may be driven away whilst the choke remains in action, but the knob should be released and pushed in gradually as the engine attains normal operating temperature.

NOTE: The accelerator pedal should not be depressed when starting from cold.

Idling: This carburettor is not provided with a separate idling circuit. The fuel is provided by the jet orifice, which is controlled by a screw at the lower end of the jet. Turning this adjusting screw clockwise weakens the mixture; turning anticlockwise will enrich it.

Normal running: When opening the throttle, manifold depression is transferred via a drilling to the vacuum chamber, which is sealed from the main body by means of a diaphragm. The difference in pressure between the vacuum chamber and the throat causes the air valve to lift. Any increase in engine speed or load will enlarge the effective choke area since the position of the air valve is proportional to the weight of air passing the throttle. Air velocity and pressure drop across the jet orifice remain approximately constant, ensuring good fuel atomization at all speeds.

The rising air valve withdraws a tapered metering needle, fitted in the base of the air valve and held by a screw from the jet orifice, increasing the flow of fuel relative to the greater air flow.

The metering needle is tapered and machined to very close limits, providing a mixture ratio for all speeds and loads in accordance with engine requirements.

Acceleration: At any point in the throttle range a temporarily richer mixture is needed at the moment the accelerator is suddenly fully depressed. To provide this, a dash-pot (hydraulic damper) is arranged inside the hollow guide rod of the air valve. This guide rod is filled with oil to within $\frac{1}{4}$in of the end of the rod in which the damper operates. Opening the throttle fully, the upward motion of the air valve is resisted by this plunger. During this time the suction or depression at the jet orifice is increased and the mixture enriched.

Adjustments:

Idling adjustments: Two adjustments are employed to vary the idle speed and mixture; to adjust, proceed as follows:

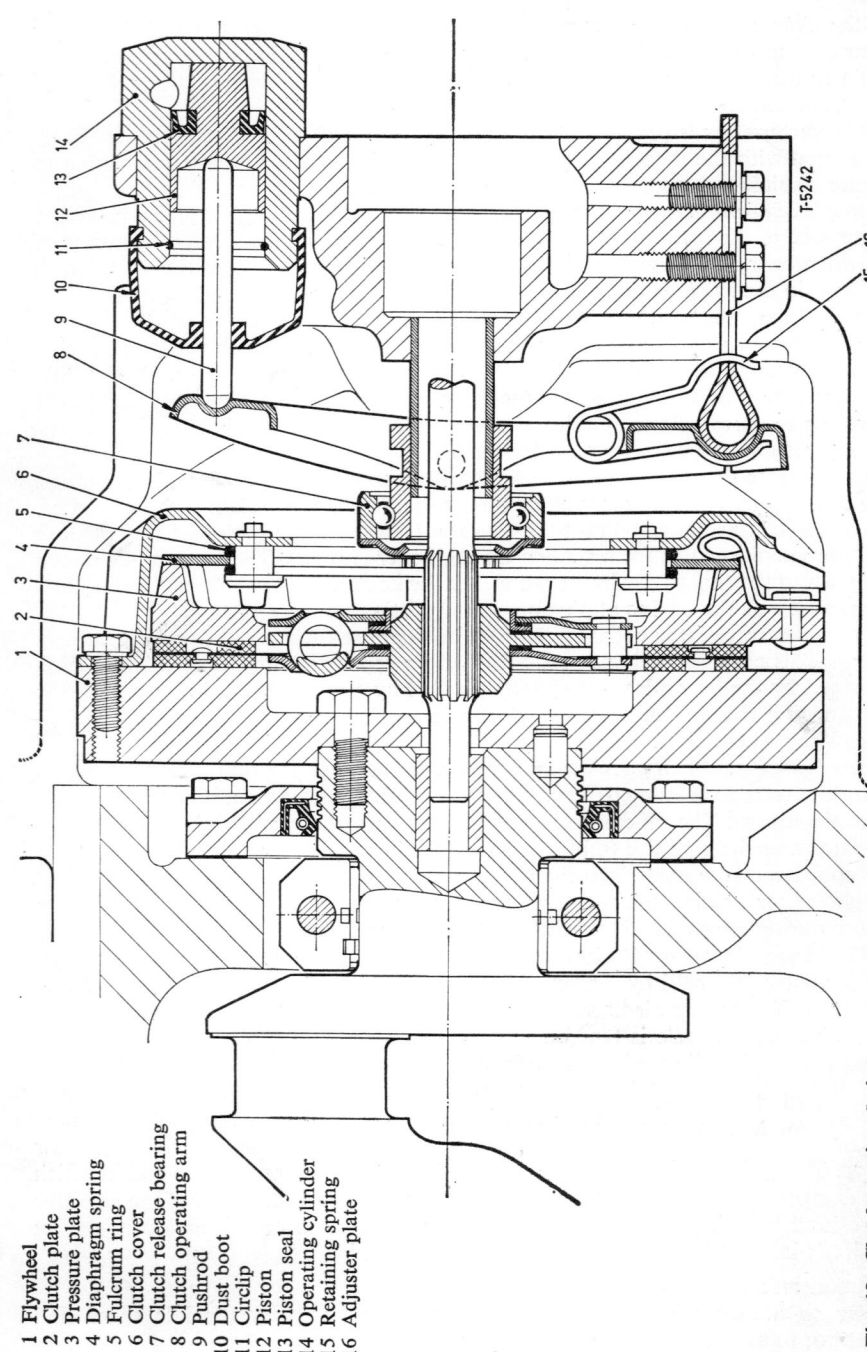

1 Flywheel
2 Clutch plate
3 Pressure plate
4 Diaphragm spring
5 Fulcrum ring
6 Clutch cover
7 Clutch release bearing
8 Clutch operating arm
9 Pushrod
10 Dust boot
11 Circlip
12 Piston
13 Piston seal
14 Operating cylinder
15 Retaining spring
16 Adjuster plate

T-5242

Fig. 18. Clutch, sectioned view

Remove the air-cleaner, hold down the air valve on to the bridge in the throttle bore. Turn the screw at the bottom of the jet until the jet is felt to contact the underside of the air valve. Turn back the screw three turns from this position. Run the engine to normal operating temperature and adjust the idle stop screw until the engine runs at 600rpm. The engine beat must be smooth and regular; the correct idle position of the jet will be determined by turning the jet adjustment screw. The adjustment may be checked by lifting the air valve with a very thin screwdriver and listening to the effect on the engine speed. If the speed rises appreciably, the mixture is too rich; if the engine stops, the mixture is too weak. When correctly adjusted, the engine speed will remain constant or fall slightly upon lifting the air valve.

NOTE: The evenness of idling depends to a large extent upon the general engine condition.

Float level: When correctly adjusted and with the carburettor inverted, the highest point of the float bottom should be 18mm above the face of the main body.

Jet centralization: The correct operation of the carburettor depends on free movement of the air valve and needle in the orifice. There is an annular clearance around the orifice bush which permits lateral adjustment of the bush and jet. Procedure:

(1) Lift the air valve and tighten the jet assembly fully.
(2) Screw up the orifice adjuster until the top of the orifice is just above the bridge.
(3) Slacken off the entire jet assembly half-a-turn to release the orifice bush.
(4) Let the air valve fall; the needle will enter the orifice and this automatically centralizes it. If necessary, help the air valve to fall by inserting a soft metal rod into the dash-pot after unscrewing the damper.
(5) Tighten the assembly slowly, checking that the needle remains free. Raise the air valve and let it fall; there should be an audible 'click'.

NOTE: Handle the needle very carefully.

Air valve/diaphragm assembly: A locating bead is moulded to both inner and outer radii of the diaphragm to ensure correct position. This must locate in the channel in the body. The diaphragm is secured to the air valve by a ring and screws with lock washers. When refitting the vacuum chamber cover, make sure that the screw holes in the cover line up with those in the main body, preventing disturbance of the diaphragm.

Air valve rod and guide: Apply a few drops of light oil to the rod before fitting; keep the air valve rod and guide clean.

Float chamber removal: An 'O' ring is fitted between the jet assembly and the float chamber spigot boss; take care when removing the float chamber not to damage the mating faces and floats.

TRANSMISSION

Clutch: Single dry plate, 6½in Borg and Beck diaphragm-type, hydraulically-operated clutch. The adjustment is obtained by altering the position of the clutch operating lever hinge plate. The clutch operating lever is operated by an actuating cylinder which is mounted on the transmission casing.

The clutch assembly, together with the flywheel and the crankshaft, is a dynamically balanced unit; when new parts are fitted to the clutch assembly, be sure this balance is not disturbed. The clutch unit must not be dismantled nor serviced for any reason. Should any fault be evident, a replacement unit must be fitted. The clutch unit can be replaced without removing the engine or transmission by withdrawing the 'quill' shaft which transmits the drive from the clutch to the transfer gear train.

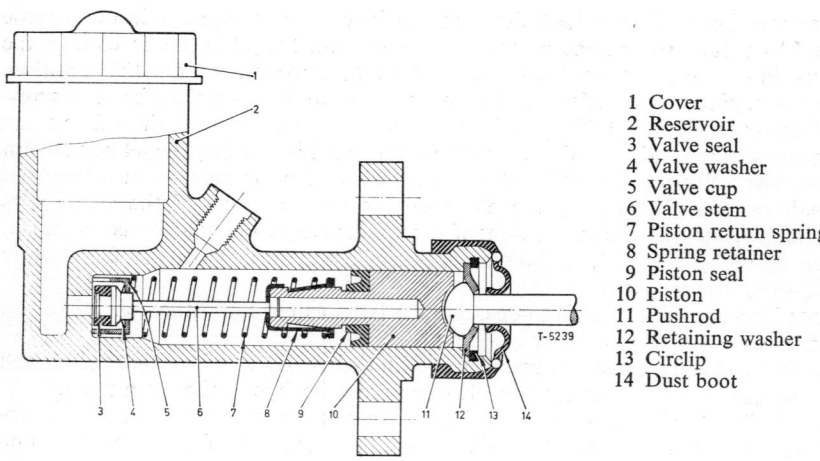

1 Cover
2 Reservoir
3 Valve seal
4 Valve washer
5 Valve cup
6 Valve stem
7 Piston return spring
8 Spring retainer
9 Piston seal
10 Piston
11 Pushrod
12 Retaining washer
13 Circlip
14 Dust boot

Fig. 19. Clutch master cylinder, sectioned view

Clutch master cylinder:

Removal and dismantling: Remove the pushrod clevis pin from the pedal, disconnect the pipe from the cylinder, after cleaning the union and the surrounding area to prevent the ingress of dirt. Catch the fluid which will now drip from the cylinder and above all be sure that no fluid drips on the paintwork of the car. Remove the two nuts securing the cylinder to the bulkhead.

Carefully slide the rubber boot from the cylinder, partly depress the pushrod and remove the circlip. Remove the pushrod and the piston assembly. Lift the lip of the spring retainer with a small screwdriver; the retainer can now be slid off the piston. The valve assembly may be taken apart by unhooking the valve stem from the slot in the spring retainer.

Thoroughly clean all parts in alcohol and blow dry with compressed air. Inspect all parts and renew those that are worn or damaged. Do not hone or polish a worn or damaged cylinder, but fit a new one. As a safety precaution, fit a new piston seal and valve seal.

Reassembly and installation: Dip the valve and piston seals in clean brake fluid and fit these to the valve and piston.

Slide the wave washer, the spacer and the spring over the valve stem in the slot in the spring retainer. Push the spring retainer over the piston and make sure that the lip snaps behind the piston boss. Moisten the cylinder bore with clean brake fluid. Dip the piston assembly in clean brake fluid and place it in the cylinder, being careful not to damage the piston seal. Insert the pushrod and push the piston down the cylinder bore part of the way. Ensure that the retainer washer is squarely seated and fit the circlip in the groove. Slide the dust boot over the cylinder, install the unit and connect the pushrod and fluid pipe. Fill the reservoir with brake fluid of the recommended type and bleed the system (see page 11).

Clutch operating cylinder:

Removal and dismantling: Remove the parcel shelf, the carpet and the transmission cover panel. Remove the parcel shelf bracket and the input shaft end-cover. Disconnect the fluid pipe from the operating cylinder and catch the fluid which will now drip from the pipe and cylinder. Above all, be sure that no fluid drips on the paintwork of the car or on the upholstery. Remove the cylinder from the transmission casing by sliding it rearwards; remove the rubber insulator pad.

Remove the dust boot and pushrod. Lift out the circlip and remove the piston and seal assembly by blowing it out of the cylinder with low-pressure compressed air. Remove the seal from the piston.

Clean the parts in alcohol and blow dry with compressed air. Inspect all parts and renew as necessary. Do not hone or polish a worn or damaged cylinder but fit a new one. As a safety precaution, fit a new piston seal.

Dip the piston and seal in clean brake fluid and assemble in reverse order of dismantling.

Re-installation is carried out in reverse order of removal. Bleed the system.

Bleeding: Clean the bleeder screw area and remove the small dust cap. Fit a length of rubber hose on the bleeder screw and hang the end in a clean container which is partly filled with brake fluid. Check the fluid level in the clutch master cylinder reservoir and top-up if necessary. During the bleeding operation the reservoir must be kept at least half full to prevent air from entering the system.

Open the bleeder screw a full turn and slowly pump the pedal until the fluid which emerges from the hose is free of air bubbles. Close the bleeder screw and top-up the reservoir with new brake fluid. Do not use the fluid which is pumped out during the bleeding operation, as this will be aerated and possibly contaminated.

Gearbox and final drive: Four-speed gearbox, fully synchronized constant mesh with helical gears. Gear-changing is effected by a centrally-mounted gear-shift lever. The final drive is integral with the gearbox, using hypoid bevel gears driving the front wheels through wide angle Rzeppa-type constant velocity joints.

Transmission removal and dismantling: Remove the engine from the car (see *Removal of the engine/transmission unit*). With the unit suspended on the hoist, remove the two long bolts and the 'O' rings from beneath the transmission casing; drain the oil. Lower the unit onto a bench. Remove the input shaft end-plate, and replace the bolts in the casing. Remove the nylon bolt, washer and rubber 'O' ring from the input shaft, and withdraw the input shaft using tools No 4235A and S.4235A–9 (impact puller and adaptor). Progressively slacken the clutch retaining bolts, and lift out the cover assembly and driven plate. Unscrew the bolts securing the engine to the transmission; separate the engine from the transmission unit.

Unscrew the locking bolt that secures the fork end to the selector/shifter shaft and remove. Remove the rear mounting and bracket and unbolt the rear end-cover. Place the end-cover assembly on the bench; remove the reverse lock plunger and spring, and the speedometer driven gear assembly. Remove the circlip and spacing washer, in order to withdraw the swinging arm assembly from the end-cover. Remove the two rubber 'O' rings.

Pull off the detent spring and unscrew the locking bolt so the selector/shifter shaft can be withdrawn. Disengage and remove the selector/shifter arm from the shifter-fork shafts by sliding it upwards.

Move the first/second shifter-fork shaft (the lower one) out by 3/32 in and slide the interlock lever plate off the sleeve.

Use a $\frac{3}{16}$ in Allen wrench to remove the socket screw, countersunk washer and locating plate from the intermediate idler gear shaft.

Remove the centre plate, using tool No. 4235A with adaptor No. S.4235A–9. Remove the countershaft gear cluster thrust springs and the shims from the top-gear pinion ball-bearing. Remove the input gear assembly; use tool No. 4235A and adaptor No. S.4235A–8 to remove the input gear roller bearing and seal.

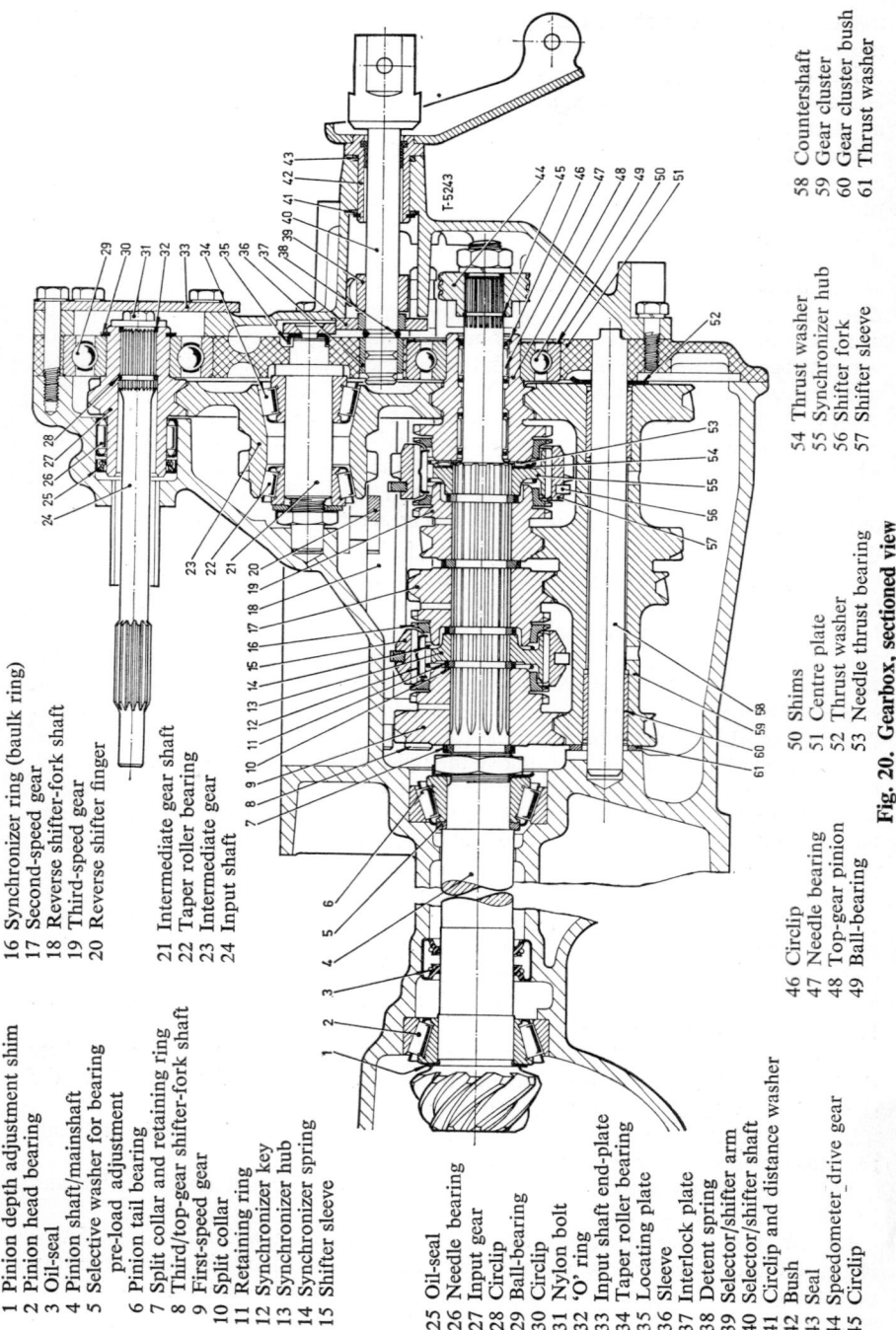

Fig. 20. Gearbox, sectioned view

1 Pinion depth adjustment shim
2 Pinion head bearing
3 Oil-seal
4 Pinion shaft/mainshaft
5 Selective washer for bearing pre-load adjustment
6 Pinion tail bearing
7 Split collar and retaining ring
8 Third/top-gear shifter-fork shaft
9 First-speed gear
10 Split collar
11 Retaining ring
12 Synchronizer key
13 Synchronizer hub
14 Synchronizer spring
15 Shifter sleeve

16 Synchronizer ring (baulk ring)
17 Second-speed gear
18 Reverse shifter-fork shaft
19 Third-speed gear
20 Reverse shifter finger
21 Intermediate gear shaft
22 Taper roller bearing
23 Intermediate gear
24 Input shaft

25 Oil-seal
26 Needle bearing
27 Input gear
28 Circlip
29 Ball-bearing
30 Circlip
31 Nylon bolt
32 'O' ring
33 Input shaft end-plate
34 Taper roller bearing
35 Locating plate
36 Sleeve
37 Interlock plate
38 Detent spring
39 Selector/shifter arm
40 Selector/shifter shaft
41 Circlip and distance washer
42 Bush
43 Seal
44 Speedometer drive gear
45 Circlip

46 Circlip
47 Needle bearing
48 Top-gear pinion
49 Ball-bearing
50 Shims
51 Centre plate
52 Thrust washer
53 Needle thrust bearing

54 Thrust washer
55 Synchronizer hub
56 Shifter fork
57 Shifter sleeve
58 Countershaft
59 Gear cluster
60 Gear cluster bush
61 Thrust washer

Unscrew the mainshaft nut, remove the lockwasher and, using a puller, withdraw the speedometer drive gear. Remove the circlip. Use tool No. 4235A and adaptor S.4235A to remove the idler assembly. If necessary, the idler assembly can be dismantled by removing the nut, tab washer, 'D' washer, taper bearing, shaft and the second taper bearing. Use tool No. 4235A and adaptor S.4235A–9 to remove the countershaft. Remove the gear cluster with its two thrust washers. If necessary, the two bushes may be removed from the ends of the gear cluster. Withdraw the top-gear pinion. Remove the circlip, washer and retaining rings to remove the two mainshaft needle bearings. Remove the synchronizer ring, needle thrust bearing, thrust washer, third/top-gear shifter-fork shaft, shifter sleeve with fork and synchronizer keys. Use tool No. S–323 and adaptor S.323–2 to withdraw the synchronizer hub and third-gear synchronizer ring. Extract the circlips from the hub and remove the retaining ring, split collar, third-speed gear, retaining ring, split collar, second-speed gear, second-gear synchronizer ring, first/second shifter-fork shaft, shifter sleeve and fork, synchronizer keys, retaining ring and split collar. Remove the socket screw and withdraw the reverse idler shaft with tool 4235A and adaptor S.4235A. Remove the reverse idler gear; if necessary, replace the bush. Drift out the retaining pin and remove the shifter finger. Withdraw the reverse shifter shaft. Using tool S.323 and adaptor S.323–2, remove the first/second synchronizer hub and first-gear synchronizer ring. Remove the retaining ring, split collar, first-speed gear, retaining ring and split collar.

Thoroughly clean and inspect all parts, replacing any that are worn or damaged. *Reassembly:* Install the countershaft in the casing. Fit the gear cluster with the two thrust washers on either side. Measure the end-float with a straight-edge placed over the mating face of the casing and a set of feeler gauges; this should be 0·003 to 0·013 in. If necessary, select new thrust washers; when the correct end-float has been obtained, remove the gear cluster and countershaft. Assemble the split collar, retaining ring, first-speed gear, split collar, retaining ring and synchronizer ring. Insert the synchronizer keys into the slots in the synchronizer hub, sliding the unit into the shifter sleeve. Fit one spring in position, invert the unit and fit the other spring so that the open ends are 120° apart. Install the synchronizer assembly in the mainshaft (long boss of hub towards open end of casing), locating the shifter fork in the groove on the shifter sleeve. With tool S.323, press the assembly along the mainshaft until it is approximately ½ in from the correctly fitted position.

At this stage line up the slots in the synchronizer ring with the synchronizer keys and also the shifter-fork shaft with its register in the end wall of the casing. Press the unit into position, ensuring that the shifter-fork shaft is correctly located. Install the reverse shifter finger; fit the reverse shifter shaft. Retain the shifter finger with the locking pin. Assemble the reverse idler gear and shaft to the casing, with the flat facing upwards. Fit the screw and tighten to 8 to 10 lb ft. Install the split collar, retaining ring, synchronizer ring, second-speed gear, split collar, retaining ring, third-speed gear, split collar, retaining ring and synchronizer ring. Fit the third/top-gear synchronizer unit onto the mainshaft, locating the shifter fork in the groove on the shifter sleeve.

With tool S.323, press the assembly along the mainshaft.

The shifter-fork groove side of the sleeve must face the same direction as the long boss of the hub, which should be facing the final drive end of the casing. When the hub is approximately ½ in from the correctly fitted position, line up the slots in the synchronizer ring with the synchronizer keys and also the shifter-fork shaft with its register in the end wall of the casing.

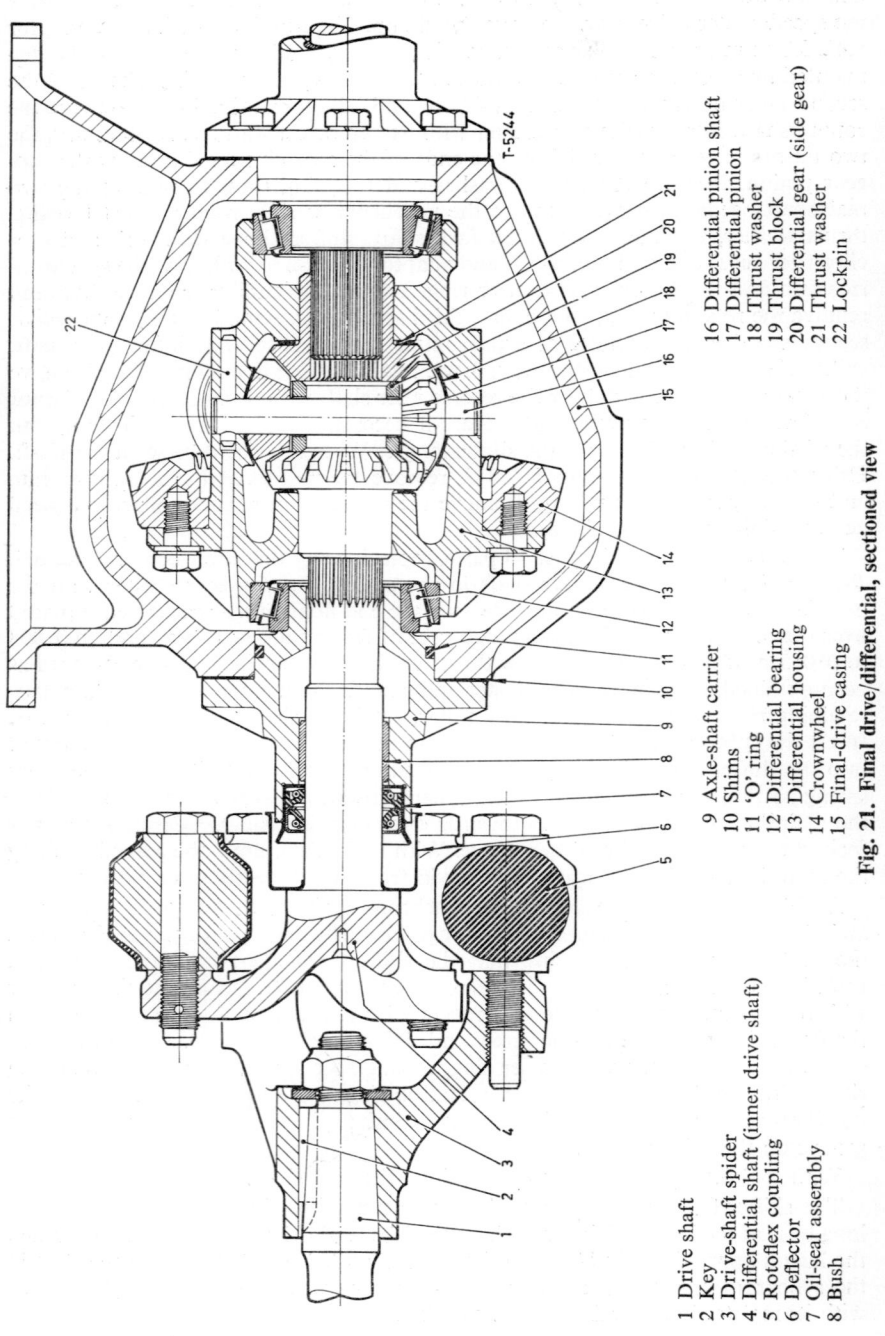

T-5244

16 Differential pinion shaft
17 Differential pinion
18 Thrust washer
19 Thrust block
20 Differential gear (side gear)
21 Thrust washer
22 Lockpin

9 Axle-shaft carrier
10 Shims
11 'O' ring
12 Differential bearing
13 Differential housing
14 Crownwheel
15 Final-drive casing

1 Drive shaft
2 Key
3 Drive-shaft spider
4 Differential shaft (inner drive shaft)
5 Rotoflex coupling
6 Deflector
7 Oil-seal assembly
8 Bush

Fig. 21. Final drive/differential, sectioned view

Hold the thrust washer and needle thrust bearing in position with grease. Install the synchronizer ring, top-gear pinion assembly and circlip. Having pressed the ball race onto the top-gear pinion boss, ensure that the needle thrust bearing is still held in position correctly and that the top gear pinion is properly seated.

Install the speedometer drive gear with the spring washer and nut.

Fit the bearing onto the intermediate idler gear shaft and fit the idler gear, bearing, 'D' washer, locking plate and nut. Check the end-float and adjust it to the specified 0·001–0·003 in, by turning the nut. When the correct end-float has been obtained, secure the nut by bending over the lock tabs. Drive the idler assembly into position with the flat on the end of the shaft facing downwards.

After checking the countershaft end-float as described above, retain one thrust washer on the machined register at the final drive end of the casing with grease. Hold the cluster gear in position and tap the spindle through the bore into the casing, ensuring that the flats on the end are horizontal. Fit the second thrust washer.

Install the input gear seal and the needle roller bearing (lettering facing outwards) using tool S.333. Fit the input gear assembly into the casing. A new sleeve can be fitted into the centre plate if necessary. Install the gear cluster springs and the shims for the top-gear pinion ball-bearing. Use a new gasket on the casing face. Carefully tap the entire plate onto the casing, making sure the needle thrust bearing has not become dislodged, causing the top-gear pinion to be incorrectly seated. Check the top-gear pinion end-float at the bearing recess of the centre plate, adjusting the shimpack to provide 0·006–0·011 in end-float if necessary. Install the interlock lever plate on the sleeve and refit the selector/shifter arm. Install the selector/shifter shaft and spring, securing the arm with the locking bolt. Install the speedometer gear assembly in the rear cover. Fit the two 'O' rings and secure the swinging arm with distance washer and circlip. Install the reverse locking plunger and spring. Using a new gasket, fit the rear cover assembly. Install the selector/shifter fork end and tighten the locking bolt. Install a new circlip to the input shaft before pressing the shaft into the input gear. Using a new gasket, install the 'O' ring, washer and nylon bolt. Fit the end-plate. Install the rear mounting and bracket. For specifications and tolerances see *Technical Data*. Refitting the transmission unit to the engine is a reversal of the removal procedure. Do not forget to replenish engine, transmission and final drive with the recommended lubricants (see page 10/11). Fill the cooling system.

Final drive: The final drive is fitted in the lower part of the transmission casing at the front. It uses hypoid bevel gears and drives the front wheels through wide angle constant velocity joints. Having removed the transmission unit from the car, dismantling of the differential unit is carried out as follows:

Dismantling: Remove the front cover and gasket, allowing the final drive oil to drain. Pull out the inner drive shafts to remove the Rotaflex couplings. Remove the axle-shaft carrier bolts; withdraw the carrier assemblies and shims supporting the weight of the differential. Clean the oil from the two differential bearings. Remove the crownwheel from the differential housing. To measure flange run-out, temporarily refit the differential unit (without the crownwheel), axle-shaft carrier assembles and shims to the casing. Maximum run-out must not exceed 0·003 in. Excessive run-out is caused by worn or damaged bearings and/or a distorted differential housing flange.

Remove the differential unit, axle shafts, carriers and shims (note thickness of shimpacks).

The differential bearings can be withdrawn if necessary using tool S.323, adaptor S.323-1 and distance piece. The seal assemblies and bushes can also be replaced. Remove the locking pin and drift out the differential pinion shaft. Rotate the two side gears so that the two differential pinions can be withdrawn through the apertures in the differential housing. Remove the thrust block, the two thrust washers, the side gears and their thrust washers. If the pinion has to be removed, dismantle the gearbox mainshaft, as described on page 35. Release the locking plate and remove the pinion/mainshaft nut. Drive out the shaft and remove the tail bearing and spacer. Use tools S.4221A and S.4221A-17 to separate the head bearing from the pinion and remove the shimpack. Remove the two seals from the casing and the pinion bearing outer races.

Clean all components; examine all parts for wear or deterioration and replace where necessary. Ensure bearing components remain in sets. Crownwheels and pinions are manufactured as matched pairs and etched with identical identification marks.

Reassembly: To ensure accurate adjustment remove all burrs and clean the mating faces of differential components. Drive the pinion bearing outer races into the casing. Install the pinion head bearing on the dummy pinion shaft (tool M84B-3) and place it in the casing. Fit the tail bearing, locking plate and nut. Use tool S.330 to tighten the nut until a torque of 12 to 16 lb/in is required to rotate the pinion.

It is best to use a suitable pre-load gauge to set the pinion bearing pre-load.

Zero the pinion-setting gauge whilst fully depressing the gauge stylus with the setting button. To determine the thickness of the shims to be fitted between the pinion head and bearing, place the gauge in the casing so that the stylus contacts the machined face of the dummy pinion. Exert a downward pressure on the gauge body and slowly rock the gauge in order to establish the point of minimum gauge reading. Add this value to the figure which is etched on the pinion to be installed; the sum of both values is the thickness of the shims needed to be fitted. (A minus figure on the pinion must be subtracted from the dial gauge reading.) Remove the gauge, dummy pinion, and bearing race from the casing.

With the aid of tool S.332 install the two oil-seals. Fit the required shims and the head bearing using tools S.4221A and S.4221A-17. Use tool S.331 to fit the seal protector. Fit the assembly into the casing with the spacer, tail bearing, locking plate and nut. Tighten the pinion nut to a torque of 100 to 110 lb ft.

Determining the pinion bearing pre-load:

Fit the pinion holding tool over the coupling muff and attach a pre-load gauge to the pinion. The torque required to rotate the pinion should be between 12 and 20 lb/in. To increase the pre-load, use a thinner spacer and to decrease use a thicker spacer. After the correct pre-load has been obtained, tighten the nut to the correct torque, securing it with the lock tab.

Fit new bushes and new bearings if necessary to the axle-shaft carriers, and carefully install the seal assemblies. Fit the thrust washers to the differential side gears, then install these in the differential housing. Stick the thrust washers with grease to the differential pinions, and insert the assemblies through the apertures in the differential housing to mesh with the sun gears. Further assembly is a reversal of the dismantling procedure.

Determining the differential pinion to side gear backlash:

This can be determined by measuring the side gear end-float with a feeler gauge. The backlash can be adjusted by using different thicknesses of differential pinion

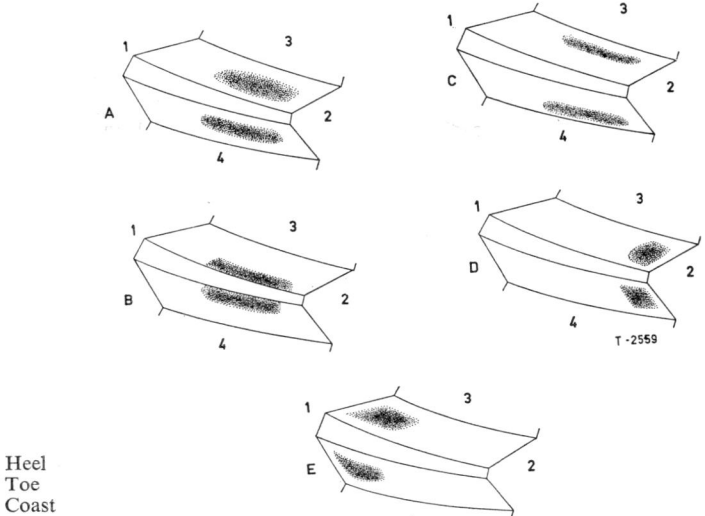

1 Heel
2 Toe
3 Coast
4 Drive
A Correct tooth contact.
B High tooth contact. Fit thicker pinion depth adjustment shim; repeat complete adjustment operation.
C Low tooth contact. Fit thinner pinion depth adjustment shim; repeat complete adjustment operation.
D Toe contact. Increase crownwheel to pinion backlash; if necessary fit thicker pinion depth adjustment shim and repeat complete adjustment operation.
E [Heel contact. Decrease crownwheel to pinion backlash; if necessary fit thinner pinion depth [adjustment shim and repeat complete adjustment operation.

Fig. 22. Final drive, tooth contacts

thrust washers or side gear thrust blocks of varying widths until an end-float of between $0·002$ in and $0·004$ in is obtained.

Determining the differential bearing pre-load:

Press in the differential bearings. Holding the differential assembly in position, install one axle-shaft carrier assembly; do not fit the adjustment shims at this stage. Secure this carrier to the casing, tightening the bolts to the requisite torque. Attach the second carrier with only three bolts, ensuring that these are all just finger-tight. Measure the gap between the axle-shaft carrier flange and the casing; let this be dimension 'A' which is needed for later adjustment. Remove the differential and axle-shaft carrier assemblies.

Fit the crownwheel to the differential housing. Using new lockwashers, tighten the attaching bolts to the requisite torque. Install the differential unit and axle-shaft carrier assemblies to the casing, but do not fit the shims at this stage. Use only three bolts on each side to secure the carriers. Progressively screw in the bolts on the crownwheel side and slacken the bolts on the other side until the crownwheel is in mesh with the pinion and all backlash has been eliminated. With the three bolts on each side finger tight, measure the gap between the axle-shaft carrier flange on the crownwheel side and the casing to produce dimension 'B'. Remove the differential and axle-shaft carrier assemblies.

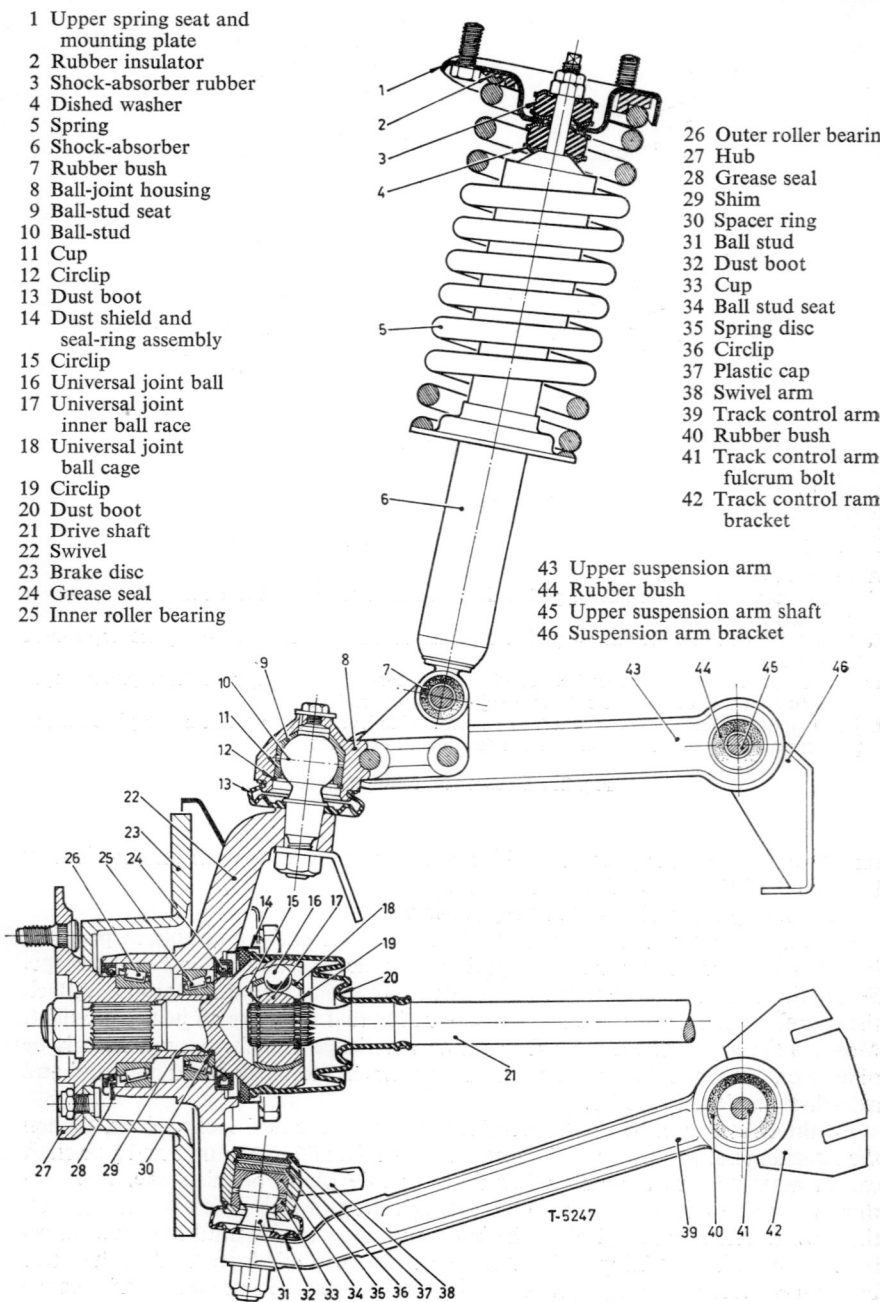

1 Upper spring seat and mounting plate
2 Rubber insulator
3 Shock-absorber rubber
4 Dished washer
5 Spring
6 Shock-absorber
7 Rubber bush
8 Ball-joint housing
9 Ball-stud seat
10 Ball-stud
11 Cup
12 Circlip
13 Dust boot
14 Dust shield and seal-ring assembly
15 Circlip
16 Universal joint ball
17 Universal joint inner ball race
18 Universal joint ball cage
19 Circlip
20 Dust boot
21 Drive shaft
22 Swivel
23 Brake disc
24 Grease seal
25 Inner roller bearing

26 Outer roller bearing
27 Hub
28 Grease seal
29 Shim
30 Spacer ring
31 Ball stud
32 Dust boot
33 Cup
34 Ball stud seat
35 Spring disc
36 Circlip
37 Plastic cap
38 Swivel arm
39 Track control arm
40 Rubber bush
41 Track control arm fulcrum bolt
42 Track control ram bracket

43 Upper suspension arm
44 Rubber bush
45 Upper suspension arm shaft
46 Suspension arm bracket

T-5247

Fig. 23. Front wheel drive and suspension, sectioned view

The correct differential bearing pre-load is obtained by accurate shimming, thus:

Example:

Dimension 'A':	0·059 in
Requisite total pre-load:	0·003 in
Subtraction gives the total shims required:	0·056 in
Shim thickness on side bearing nearest crownwheel–	
Dimension 'B':	0·020 in
Requisite backlash (0·004 to 0·006 in):	0050· in
Addition gives the total shims required on this side:	0·025 in
Shim thickness on side bearing furthest from crownwheel–	
Dimension 'A', minus pre-load:	0·056 in
Shim thickness on crownwheel side bearing:	0·025 in
Subtraction gives the thickness of shims on this side:	0·031 in

After the 'O' rings and appropriate shims have been fitted onto the carrier flanges, assemble the axle-shaft carrier assemblies and the differential unit. Tighten the bolts to the correct torque. The backlash between the crownwheel and the pinion should now be measured at several points by means of a dial indicator mounted on the transmission casing cover mounting flange, its index resting at a right-angle to the flank of a crownwheel tooth. The backlash should be between 0·004 in to 0·006 in; if necessary, correction can be made by moving shims behind the differential bearings with the corrective thickness from one side of the differential to the other, until the backlash is within given limits, without changing the total shim thickness. After final assembly it is good practice to check all adjustments with the aid of Prussian or 'mechanic's blue' by examining the tooth contact pattern.

Fit the gasket, front cover, securing bolts and lock washers. Slide the inner drive shafts into position.

CHASSIS

Chassis: The body and chassis are welded together to form a single unit. The front and rear suspension assemblies are each mounted on a detachable sub-frame by means of flexible rubber mountings.

Front suspension: Independent front suspension, employing rubber-bushed upper wishbones and lower track control arms; the longitudinal position of each track control arm is determined by a stay rod, fitted between the track control arm and the sub-frame. The combined coil spring and telescopic shock-absorber units operate on the upper wishbones. The upper end of each spring and shock-absorber unit is located in the spring turret, a reinforced housing which is integral with the body shell, accessible through the bonnet aperture. The front hub and disc brake assembly is attached to a kingpost which swivels on upper and lower ball-joints at the outer ends of the top wishbones and lower suspension arms. The suspension arms are rubber-bushed at the inner end. Toe-out, caster and camber can be adjusted if necessary.

Removal of front spring and shock-absorber assembly: Place the car on stands under the centre of the sub-frame crossmember and remove the wheel. Detach the bottom of the shock-absorber from the upper wishbone; release the top of the spring unit from the turret in the body by removing the three bolts.

Remove the spring and damper assembly.

Fit a spring compressor over as many coils as possible and compress the spring

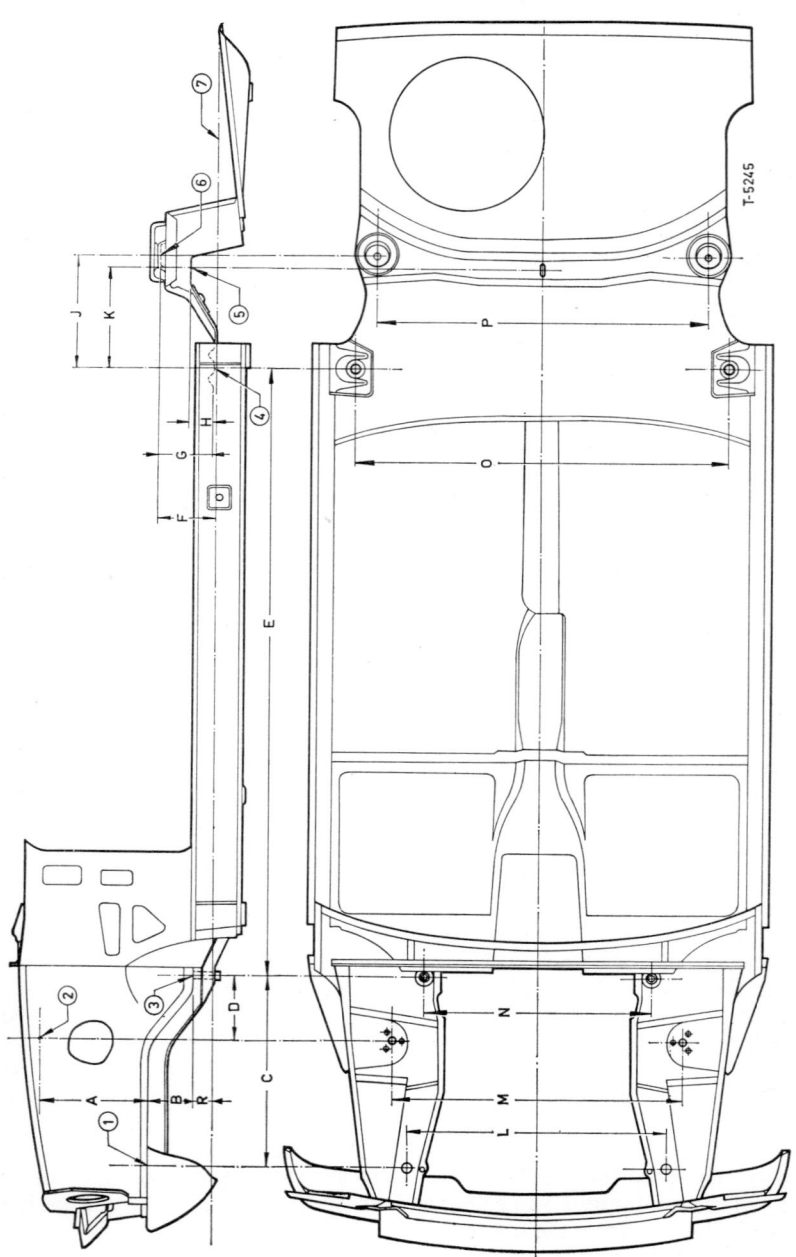

Fig. 24. Chassis/body floor dimensions

T-5246-A

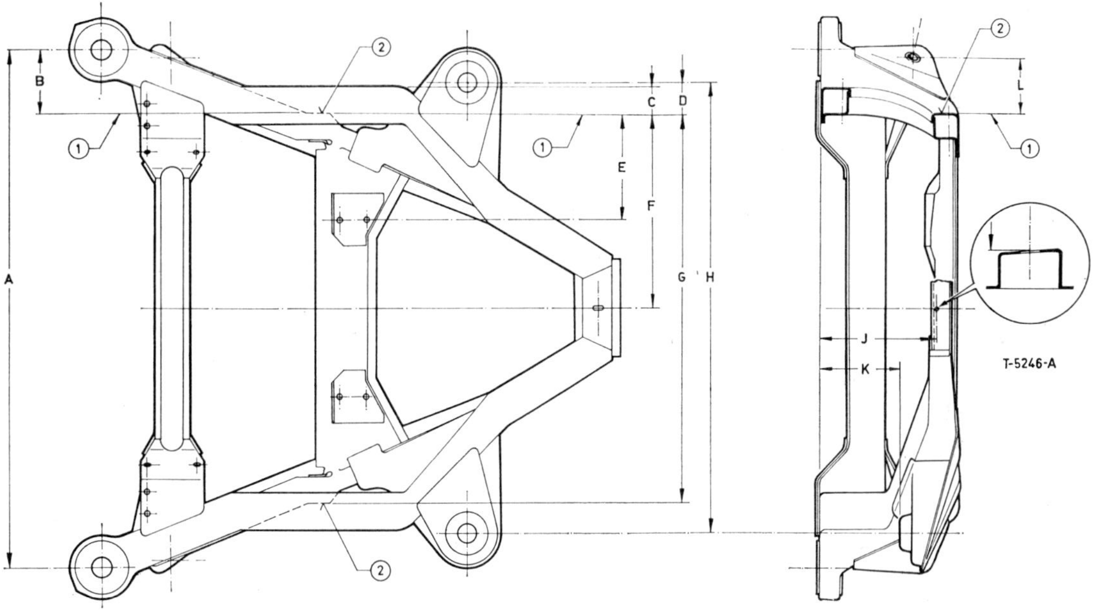

Fig. 25a. Front subframe dimensions

Key to Fig. 24 (page 42)

1 through 7: datum lines

A 12·33 in.
B   5·28 in.
C 21·35 in.
D   7·40 in.
E 70·59 in.
F   7·21 in.
G   7·02 in.
H   3·44 in.
J 12·64 in.
K 11·29 in.
L 30·20 in.
M 36   in.
N 26·50 in.
O 43·58 in.
P 38·74 in.
R   2·37 in.

Key to Fig. 25a

A 30·20 in.
B   3·57 in.
C   1·47 in.
D   1·72 in.
E   6·256 in.
F 11·53 in.
G 23·06 in.
H 26·50 in.
J   6·95 in.
K   5·01 in.
L   3·19 in.
1 is datum line
2 is datum face

D

Key to Fig. 25*b*
A 43·74in.
B 11·29in.
C 7·67in.
D 25·625in.
E 3·65in.
F 28·08in.
G 1·25in.
H 13·825in.
J 5·20in.
K 8·63in.
L 3·80in.

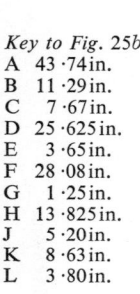
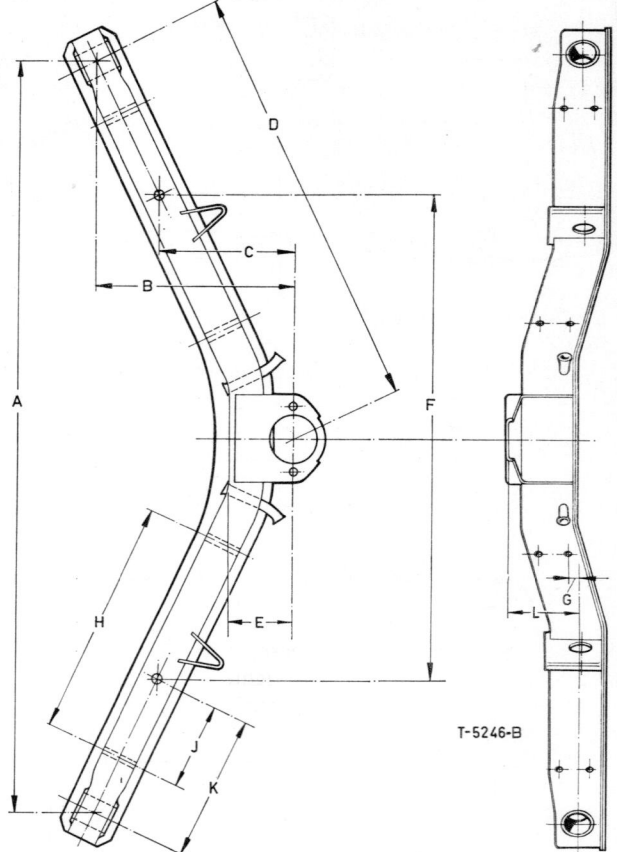

T-5246-B

Fig. 25b. Rear subframe dimensions

until the upper shock-absorber nuts can be removed. Release the spring compressor after having removed the upper spring seat; remove the spring from the shock-absorber.

Reassembly and installation are carried out in reverse order of removal and dismantling.

NOTE: Do not tighten the lower shock-absorber to wishbone attaching bolt until the weight of the car, laden with 150lb in each front seat, is resting on the front wheels; this precaution is necessary to avoid distortion of the lower shock-absorber bush.

If necessary, the upper and/or lower front suspension arms may be removed for re-bushing. After refitting, be sure to have the static laden weight of the car, with 150lb in each front seat, resting on the wheels, before the bolts and nuts are finally tightened, thus avoiding distortion of the rubber bushes.

Steering swivel and hub assembly, with drive shaft; removal and dismantling.

Front wheel hubs and bearings: The front wheel hubs run on adjustable inner and outer roller bearings. The hubs are kept in place by the separate drive flanges, which are fitted to the drive shafts by means of a Nyloc nut. The space between the inner roller bearing and the drive shaft is maintained by a spacer and shim, which creates the requisite bearing end-float.

Dismantling: Raise the front of the car onto stands and remove the wheels. Place a jack under the kingpost and remove the spring and shock-absorber unit as described above. By adjusting the jack, align the outer drive shaft with the inner one. Use tool No. S.328 to compress the Rotoflex coupling, whilst unscrewing the three bolts to detach it from the axle-shaft spider. Leave the clamp on the inner shaft. Remove the brake caliper and hose support bracket from the kingpost. Support the weight of the brake caliper to avoid distortion of the brake hose. Remove the two bolts to release the upper wishbone arms from the top ball-joint housing. Use a ball-joint extractor to carefully separate the steering tie-rod end ball-pin from the steering arm and the steering arm from the lower track control arm. Remove the kingpost/drive-shaft assembly from the car and clean.

Press out the constant velocity joint assembly from the hub and press off the kingpost. Remove the outer oil-seal and bearing, using tool S.323 and adaptor S.323–1. Remove the water shield, inner oil seal and bearing, and drift out both bearing cups.

Assembly and adjustment: Measure the difference between the wheel flange and gauge spacer, taken from tool No. S.325. Install the brake disc. Fit the kingpost with the bearings, without grease, and assemble the end-float gauge (tool No. S.325). Seat the bearings by tightening and rotating the finger screw of the tool. Insert the previously determined thickness of feeler gauges, and use a spacer and shim which are a tight fit. Their thickness would produce a dry bearing end-float of $0 \cdot 002$ in to $0 \cdot 005$ in. The gauge will show the total thickness required, which equals the space plus the specified end-float with dry bearings.

Remove the gauge, grease and refit the outer bearing. Install the outer seal, using the outer oil-seal replacing tool No. S.322 with handle No. 550. Use drift S.324 to fit the assembly to the wheel flange. Liberally grease, and tap the inner bearings onto the flange. Install the oil-seal and water shield.

Install the required spacer and shim on the stub-axle of the constant velocity joint housing and retain with grease. Tap the stub through the wheel flange until the hub nut can be engaged. Tighten the nylon nut to the specified torque and keep turning the kingpost to seat the bearings. Ensure that the wheel flange is not inverted until the bearings are in their final position, so that the outer oil-seal does not get damaged. The flange should rotate freely.

To refit the outer drive shaft and front hub assembly is a reversal of the dismantling procedure.

Constant velocity joints: The Birfield 75 AC constant velocity universal joints fitted to the outboard ends of the drive shafts are packed with grease and sealed at manufacture. The joints should be examined from time to time to check the condition of the gaiter seals. If a gaiter has been damaged, allowing the lubricant to escape, or water or dirt to enter, the gaiters must be renewed. To carry this out, the joint and shaft assembly must be removed as described above under 'front wheel hubs'.

Front wheel alignment (*see also Technical Data*):

Caster: The caster angle is decreased or increased by adding or removing washers between the boss on the inner end of the stay rod and the rubber block at the outside of the sub-frame.

Camber: The camber angle is decreased or increased by removing or adding camber shims between the upper wishbone bracket and the sub-frame.

Toe-out: The camber angle is decreased or increased by removing or adding camber shims between the upper wishbone bracket and the sub-frame.

Toe-out: Toe-out is adjusted in the usual way by shortening or lengthening the tie-rods.

Before checking and/or adjusting the front wheel alignment, ensure that the tyres are inflated to the correct pressure (see page 11) and place the car on a perfectly level floor or alignment fixture.

Steering lock is determined by the position of the tie-rods on the steering rack. The adjustment of the tie-rods is therefore of the utmost importance. See Fig. 26 for dimensions.

Steering gear: The rack and pinion steering gear is fitted to the front sub-frame by means of rubber mountings.

Removal: Raise the front of the car onto stands and remove both front wheels. Disconnect the tie-rod ends from the steering arms. Remove the 'U' bolts securing the steering rack housing to the sub-frame and remove the three clamping bolts from the steering column coupling. Detach the earthing wire from the pinion housing and remove the coupling. Use a jack under the differential casing to raise the engine $\frac{1}{2}$ in so that the rack can be withdrawn through the driver's side of the sub-frame.

Installation: Installation is a reversal of the removal operation. Always fit new mounting rubbers and do not over-tighten the 'U' bolts.

Dismantling: Release the clips and slide both gaiters outwards. Slacken the locknuts and unscrew the tie-rods from the steering rack. Remove the coil springs from each end of the rack housing. Bend back the washer tab; unscrew the sleeve and remove the tab washer, shims and thrust pad. Loosen the locknuts and unscrew the outer ball-joint assemblies from the tie-rods. Remove the locknut, gaiters, clips and cup nuts from the tie-rods. Remove the locknuts from the end of the steering rack. Unscrew the capnut and remove the shims, spring and pressure pad from the housing. Remove the set screws and withdraw the pinion assembly. Remove the rubber 'O' ring from the retainers groove. Remove the rack from the tube. Clean and examine all parts, replacing those that are worn or damaged.

If necessary remove the bush in the end of the rack housing by drifting out the old one and pressing in the new bush.

Assembly and adjustment: Insert the steering rack into the tube and fit the pinion. Adjust the pinion end-float as follows:

Fit the thrust pad and cap nut to the tube. Tighten the plug just enough to eliminate all end-float. Use a feeler gauge to measure the clearance between the cap nut and the rack housing. Remove the cap nut and thrust pad and fit a shim-pack equal in thickness to the measured gap, plus a nominal value of 0.004 in, representing the requisite clearance. Pack the unit with grease, after which further assembly is a reversal of the dismantling operation.

When correctly adjusted, a force of 2 lb at a radius of 8 in is required to rotate the pinion shaft in either direction, through three-quarters of a turn, starting from the mid-way position. This force should under no circumstances be in excess of

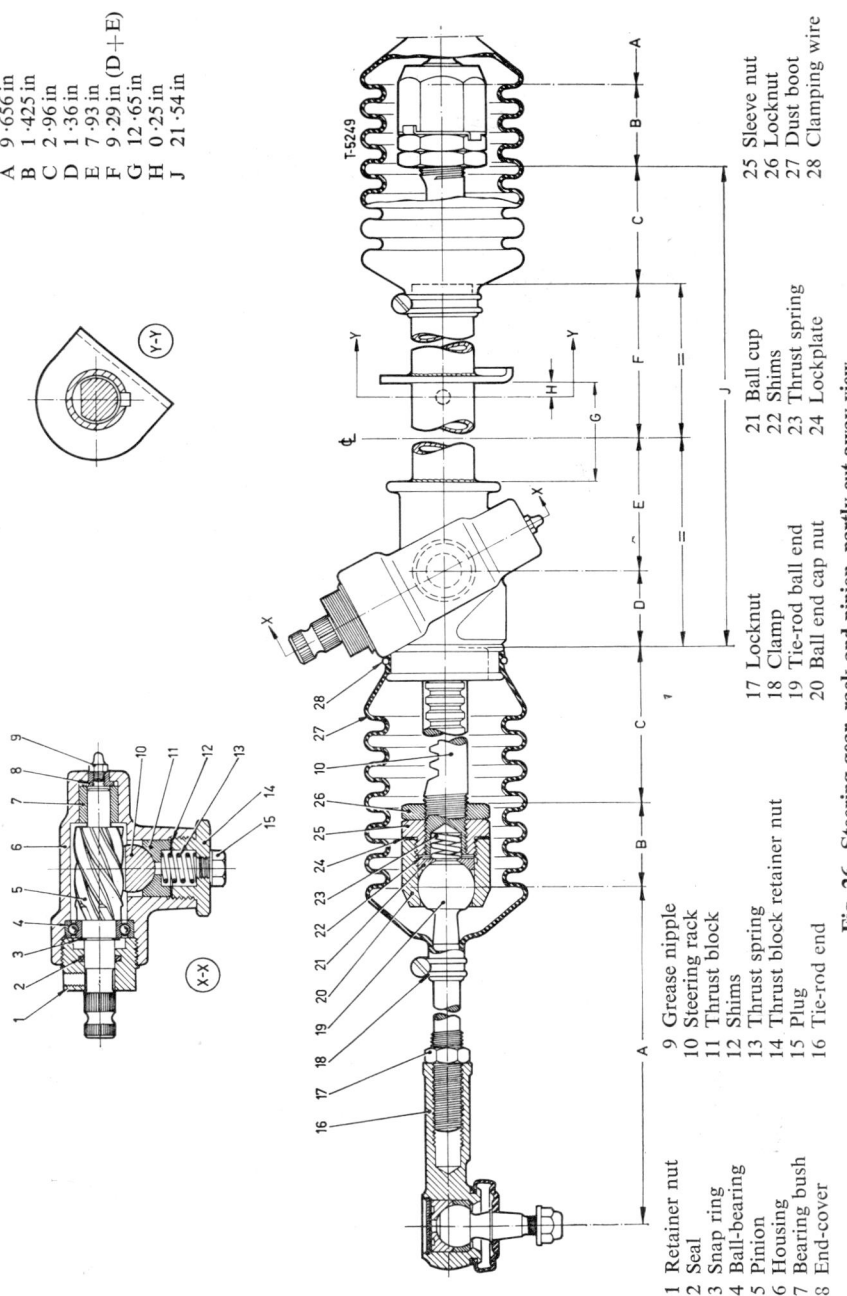

A 9·656 in
B 1·425 in
C 2·96 in
D 1·36 in
E 7·93 in
F 9·29 in (D+E)
G 12·65 in
H 0·25 in
J 21·54 in

T-5249

Fig. 26. Steering gear, rack and pinion, partly cut-away view

1 Retainer nut
2 Seal
3 Snap ring
4 Ball-bearing
5 Pinion
6 Housing
7 Bearing bush
8 End-cover
9 Grease nipple
10 Steering rack
11 Thrust block
12 Shims
13 Thrust spring
14 Thrust block retainer nut
15 Plug
16 Tie-rod end
17 Locknut
18 Clamp
19 Tie-rod ball end
20 Ball end cap nut
21 Ball cup
22 Shims
23 Thrust spring
24 Lockplate
25 Sleeve nut
26 Locknut
27 Dust boot
28 Clamping wire

1 Grommet
2 Steering column tube
3 Pinch nut
4 Snap ring
5 Spring seat washer
6 Spring
7 Ball-bearing
8 Upper steering column shaft
9 Lower steering column shaft
10 Seal
11 Dust boot
12 Dust boot sleeve
13 Spline guard sleeve
14 Column head
15 Upper ball-bearing
16 Cancelling cam for direction-indicator switch
17 Clamping blocks
18 Spring
19 Clamp bolt
20 Clamp bolt nut with knurled knob

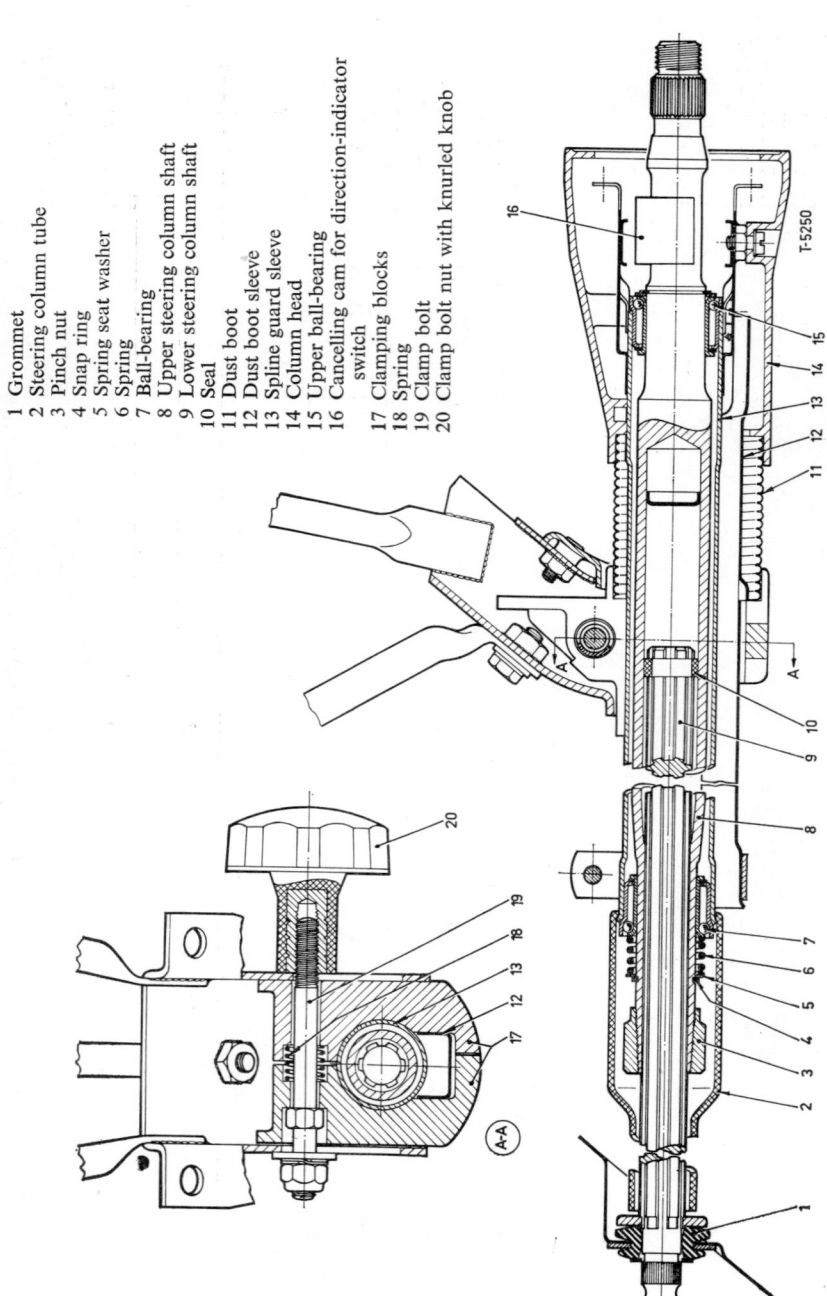

T-5250

Fig. 27. Steering column and adjustment mechanism

3 lb for the rest of the rack travel.

NOTE: When assembled, the tie-rod ball-joints should move freely in their joints. Any looseness or binding must be overcome by adding or subtracting shims to the shimpack within, respectively.

Tie-rods: The tie-rods are connected at their outer ends to the wheel swivel arms by means of non-adjustable ball-joints. The tie-rod length is adjustable in order to correct toe-in. Make sure they are adjusted to equal lengths (see Fig. 26).

Steering column: The adjustable steering column is designed to telescope. The adjustment range of 4 in axially and 2 in vertically is controlled by the column support bracket mounted handwheel. The telescopic inner column cannot be dismantled and it is recommended that in the unusual event of excessive wear occuring in the ball-bearings, the complete assembly should be replaced.

Rear suspension: Independent rear suspension with cast-aluminium semi-trailing arms, controlled by telescopic dampers co-axial with the springs. The rear suspension arms pivot on rubber bushes, situated in the detachable rear sub-frame, which is attached to the body with three flexible rubber mountings.

Removal of a rear spring: Loosen the wheel nuts and lift the rear of the car by placing a trolley jack beneath the sub-frame crossmember. Lower the car on to suitable chassis stands, ensuring that sub-frame is clear. Raise the suspension by placing a jack under the suspension arm; remove the wheel, fit spring hooks over the spring coils and disconnect the lower shock-absorber mounting. Lower the arm until the spring is just free, taking care not to stretch the hydraulic brake hose. Remove the spring and compress it to remove the hooks.

Installation is a direct reversal of the removal procedure.

Removal of a rear shock-absorber: Take out the trim panel at the back of the luggage boot and disconnect the top mounting. Remove the three lower mounting bolts and withdraw the shock-absorber downwards.

Removal of the rear sub-frame: Remove both rear springs as described above; drain the hydraulic brake system and disconnect the rear brake hoses.

Disconnect the parking brake cable at the centre joint and remove the exhaust tail-pipe. Take the weight of the sub-frame on a suitable jack and detach the three mountings securing the assembly to the body. Lower the assembly to the floor.

Installation is a reversal of the removal procedure. Do not forget to re-fill with brake fluid and bleed the hydraulic brake system.

Rear wheel hubs and bearings: The rear wheel hubs run on adjustable single roller bearings. Adjustment for new bearings is effected as follows:

Fit the hub with the bearings, without grease and grease-seal. Fit the bearing retaining washer and castellated nut. Tighten the nut sufficiently to take up all bearing end-float without causing the bearing to pinch. Mark the bearing retaining washer in relation to the nut and remove the hub. Fit a new grease-seal, fill the bearings with grease and reinstall the assembly; tighten the castellated nut until the markings coincide, then fit the split-pin. If necessary, the nut may be slackened off to line up with the nearest split-pin hole in the stub axle. Service adjustment is effected by slowly tightening the nut to not more than 5 ft lb while turning the hub; slacken the nut to the nearest hole and fit a new split-pin.

Brakes: Hydraulically-operated foot brake acting on all four wheels. The front wheels are fitted with Girling disc brakes, the rear wheels with Girling drum brakes. The parking brake operates mechanically on the rear wheels.

Front disc brakes: The Girling disc brake consists of an 8¾ in brake disc and a cast-iron double-acting caliper containing two friction pads, one on each side of the disc.

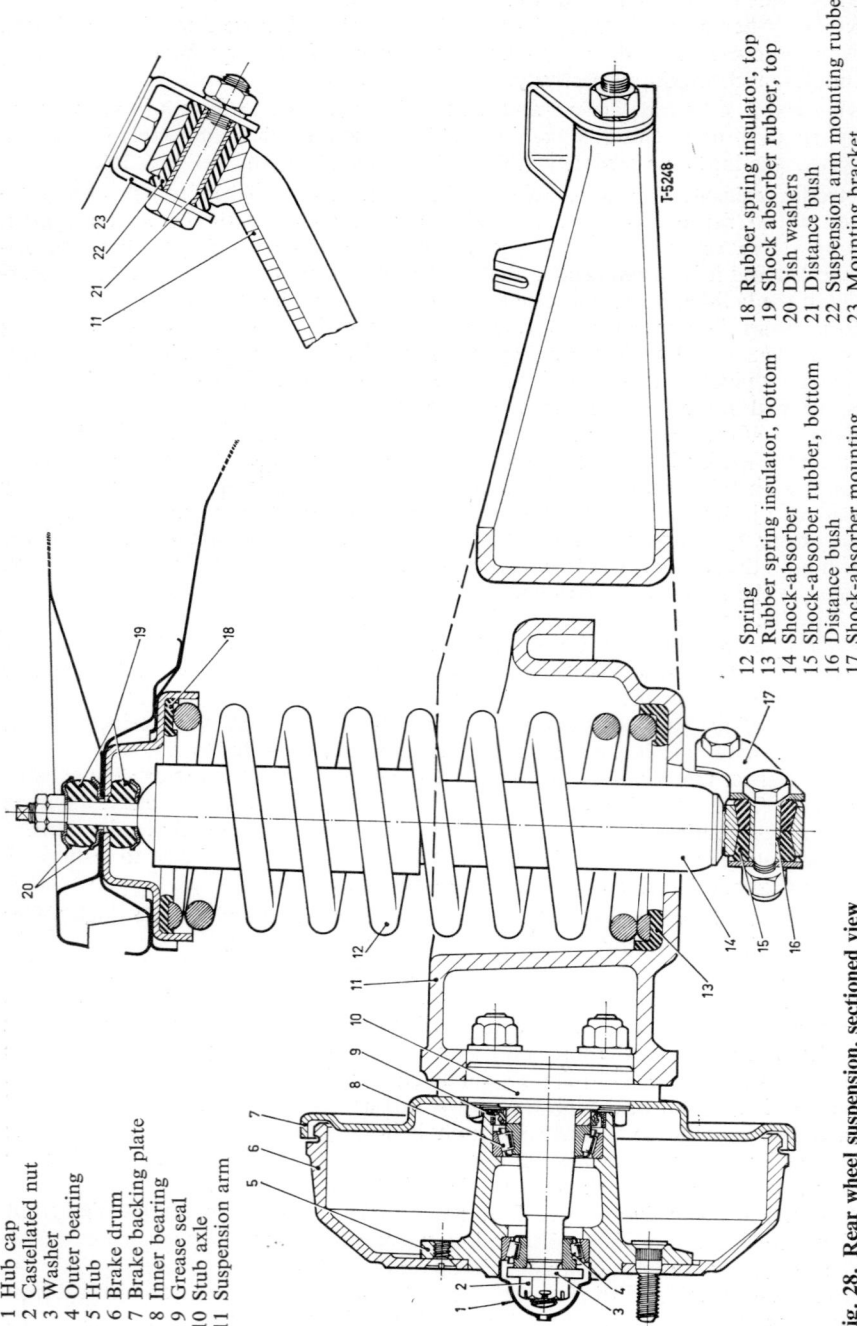

1 Hub cap
2 Castellated nut
3 Washer
4 Outer bearing
5 Hub
6 Brake drum
7 Brake backing plate
8 Inner bearing
9 Grease seal
10 Stub axle
11 Suspension arm

12 Spring
13 Rubber spring insulator, bottom
14 Shock-absorber
15 Shock-absorber rubber, bottom
16 Distance bush
17 Shock-absorber mounting

18 Rubber spring insulator, top
19 Shock absorber rubber, top
20 Dish washers
21 Distance bush
22 Suspension arm mounting rubber
23 Mounting bracket

T-5248

Fig. 28. Rear wheel suspension, sectioned view

Fig. 29. Front disc brake, installed, viewed from rear

If the thickness of the friction material on the brake pads has worn down to a thickness of $\frac{1}{8}$ in new pads should be inserted into the caliper. In order to replace the friction pads, lift the front of the vehicle and remove the relevant wheel; release the spring retainer and withdraw the pad retaining pin, and remove the pads and shims, interposed between them and the pistons. When renewing the friction pads, these shims should be replaced as well with the arrows pointing in the direction of forward wheel rotation. Before inserting the new friction pads, the exposed part of the pistons and brake-pad recesses in the caliper must be cleaned, following which the pistons should be pushed back into the cylinders. Prevent overflow of the brake fluid reservoir by syphoning off surplus fluid if necessary.

After installation, pump the brakes several times in order to bring the pads closer to the disc; spin the brake discs several times to ensure that they do not drag.
NOTE : Never depress the brake pedal whilst the friction pads are removed.

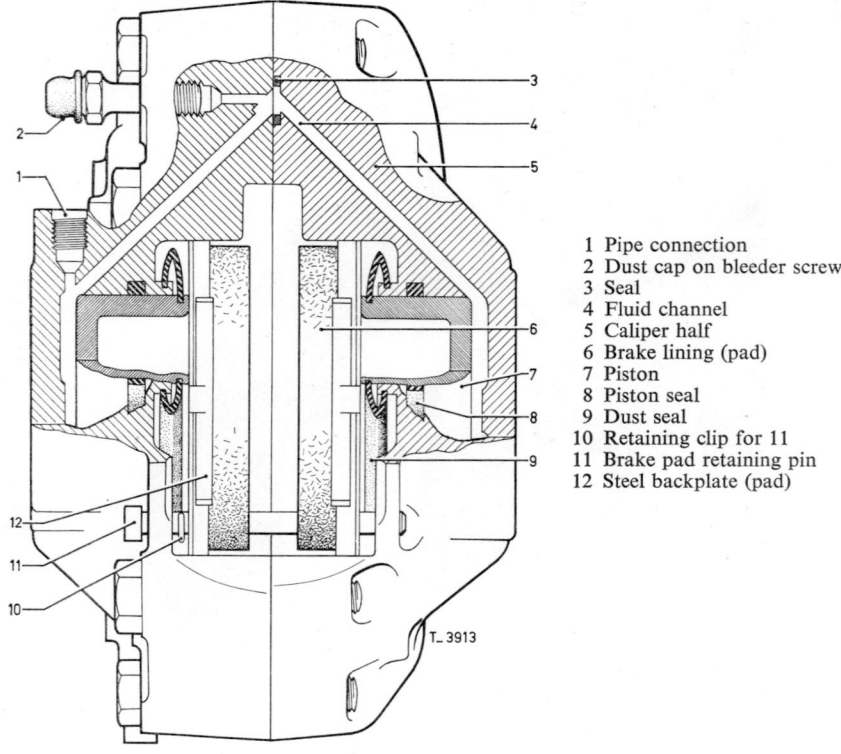

1 Pipe connection
2 Dust cap on bleeder screw
3 Seal
4 Fluid channel
5 Caliper half
6 Brake lining (pad)
7 Piston
8 Piston seal
9 Dust seal
10 Retaining clip for 11
11 Brake pad retaining pin
12 Steel backplate (pad)

T_ 3913

Fig. 30. Front disc brake caliper, sectioned view

Rear brakes: The Girling drum brake consists of an 8 in brake drum with leading and trailing brake shoes and one adjuster.

When assembling the rear brake shoes, ensure that the 'bare' end of each brake shoe is the leading end. Insert the web of one shoe into the slots in one piston and adjustment anchor and, by pulling on the opposite shoe stretch the brake shoe return springs which should be fitted as shown in Fig. 31, so that the second brake shoe can be hooked similarly to the first shoe. The layout of the various parts of the brake cylinder is also shown.

NOTE: In Fig. 31 the left rear brake is shown; the right rear brake is of the opposite hand.

Adjustment of the rear brakes: The rear brakes are adjusted by turning the square-headed adjusting screw on the inside of the brake backing-plate at the top. First screw in the adjuster until the drum is fully locked; then back-off just sufficiently to let the drum rotate freely.

NOTE: The parking brake is also adjusted by this operation unless stretched cables necessitate further adjustment.

Brake master cylinder: The brake master cylinder is mounted on the bulkhead and incorporates the brake fluid reservoir.

Removal and installation: Before removing the master cylinder, ensure that the system is drained. Disconnect the pressure pipe union and remove the unit after

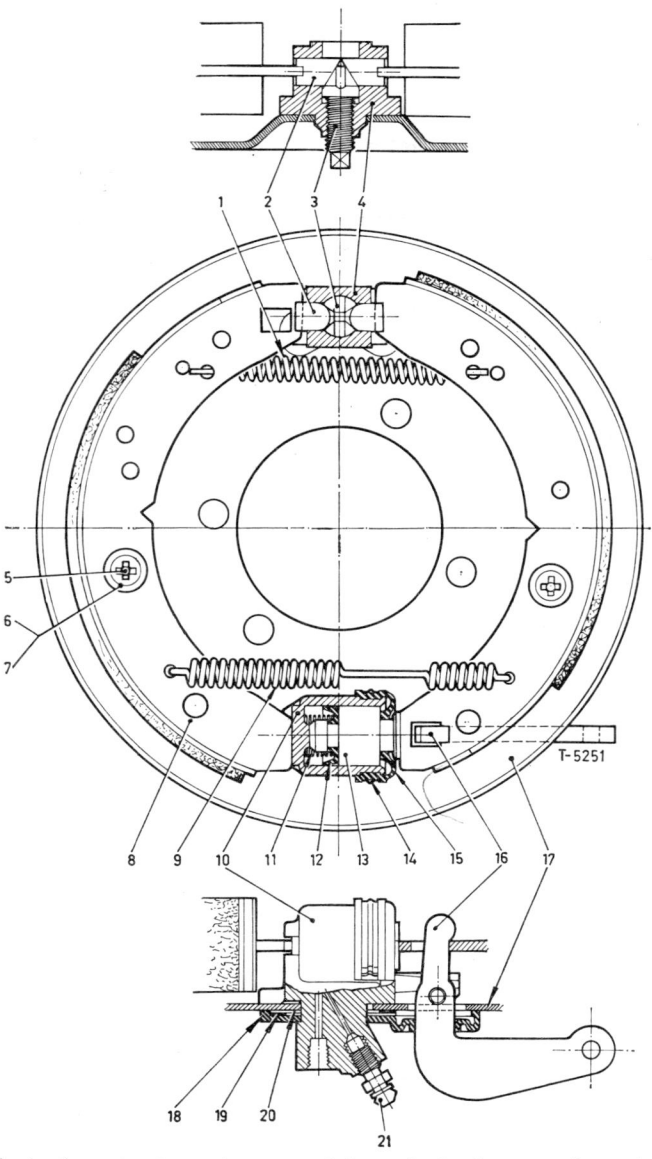

1 Upper brake shoe retracting spring
2 Adjuster tappet
3 Adjuster bolt head
4 Adjuster housing
5 Brake shoe hold-down pin
6,7 Hold-down spring and seat assembly
8 Brake shoe

9 Lower brake shoe retracting spring
10 Brake cylinder
12 Cup
13 Piston
14 Dust boot clamp
15 Dust boot
16 Parking brake lever

17 Brake backing plate
18 Dust boot
19 Abutment plate
20 Spring plate
21 Bleeder screw

Fig. 31. Rear drum brake

1 Cover
2 Reservoir
3 Valve Seal
4 Valve washer
5 Valve cup
6 Valve stem
7 Piston return spring
8 Spring retainer
9 Piston seal
10 Piston
11 Pushrod
12 Retaining washer
13 Circlip
14 Dust boot

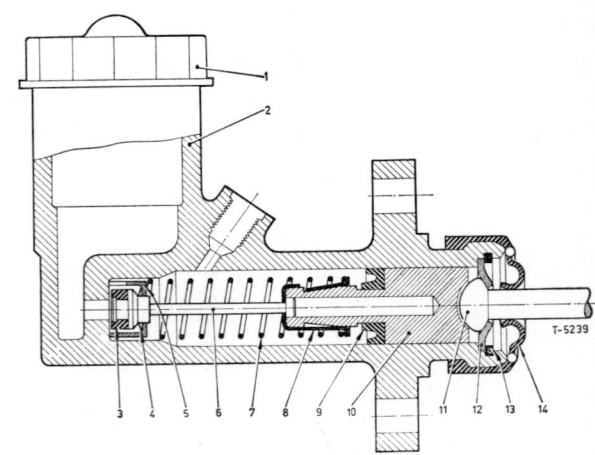

Fig. 32. Brake master cylinder, sectioned view

unscrewing its two attachment nuts and the clevis pin. Be sure that no fluid drips
on the paintwork.

Installation is a direct reversal of the above operation. Be sure to fill the brake
fluid container with the recommended brake fluid, and to bleed the hydraulic
system.

Dismantling: Remove the dust cover and depress the push-rod to remove the
circlip. Then remove the push-rod assembly. Remove the plunger and valve
assembly. Lift the locating clip to release the spring retainer, spring and valve
assembly from the plunger. Release the valve shank from the spring retainer and
remove the spring, distance piece and spring washer. Remove the seals from the
valve shank and the plunger. Wash all parts in special cleaning fluid, and replace
worn or damaged parts.

Reassembly: Ensure maximum cleanliness when reassembling the unit in reverse
order of dismantling. Before assembly, all parts should be immersed in clean brake
fluid and assembled while still wet. Tighten the bleeder screw, refill the hydraulic
system with the recommended brake fluid, and bleed the brakes.

BODY

Lock and window mechanism of front door:

Removal: Remove the wood capping by unscrewing the three securing screws.
Unscrew the armrest attaching screws and remove the armrest. Next remove
the window regulator handle and the centre trim by unscrewing the attaching
screws. Release the door-trim panel by carefully lifting the retainer clips. Release
the remote-control linkage by removing the spring clip and washer. Prise the
moulded rubber strip clear of the rear window channel; remove the lower securing
screw from the inner trailing edge of the door's box section and pull the channel
down to disengage the tongues. Unscrew the three screws and disengage the latch
mechanism from the lock; withdraw the lock.

Remove the three screws from the glass stop; remove the stop. Release the anti-
drum stiffening strip by removing the three screws. Remove the lower screw to
release the leading vent channel. Lower the window to release the regulator arm

from the lower channel. Prise off the inner and outer weather strips. Disengage the glass from the leading vent runner; tip the glass to manoeuvre clear.

Lift away a length of door sealing rubber; drill out the two rivets securing the vent pane assembly to the front edge of the door. Remove the glass sealing rubber from the top of the frame; remove the complete vent pane assembly.

Reassembly: Reassembly is carried out in reverse order of removal; replace the drilled-out rivets in the front edge of the door by pop rivets.

Lock and window mechanism of rear door: Removal and reassembly of the rear door window and lock mechanism is essentially the same as described for the front door; the essential difference is that the rear door is not equipped with a vent pane assembly but a quarterlight.

Dashboard, instrument panel:
Removal and installation: Disconnect the battery. Lower the steering column to its lowest position. Depress the pin to remove the choke control knob and unscrew the bezel. Detach the cable from the rear of the speedometer and remove the screw holding the trip controlling cable bracket. Remove the two main securing screws from either side of the instrument panel and withdraw the unit from the facia. To remove from the vehicle, carefully detach all electrical connections and screenwasher pipes. Installation is a reversal of the removal procedure, using the wiring diagram and colour code list to correctly reconnect the electrical connections.

Windscreen-wiper motor:
Removal and installation: Disconnect the battery cables and the wiring from the wiper motor. Remove the wiper arm locating screws, remove the arms and blades. Unscrew the wheel box securing nuts. Remove the parcel shelf and lower the steering column to its lowest position. Remove the facia and withdraw the mill-board cover. Unbolt the six bolts securing the mounting plate to release the whole assembly. The wiper motor can be removed from the mounting plate by removing the linkage spring clip and the three bolts.

Installation is a reversal of the removal operation. However, during reassembly, ensure that the motor earthing strip contacts one of the mounting plate.

Heater blower motor:
Removal and installation: Disconnect the battery cables and the blower motor wiring. Remove the two air-hose clips and pull off the hose. Remove the blower motor bolts from the mounting brackets and lift the unit clear.

Installation is a direct reversal of the removal operation. Ensure that the motor earthing tag is properly bolted down.

ELECTRICAL EQUIPMENT

Electrical system: 12-volt, negative (—) battery terminal earthed.

Generator:
Dismantling: After removal, the generator can be dismantled as follows:

Remove the retaining nut, extract the driving pulley and remove the Woodruff key. Remove the two long through-bolts and remove the commutator end-cover from the yoke. Note the fibre thrust washer adjacent to the commutator. Withdraw the armature and pulley end-cover complete with bearing. Support the bearing retaining plate and press the armature shaft from the pulley end-cover. If necessary, the field coils can be removed by unsoldering the field coil connections and drilling-out the rivet securing the field terminal assembly to the yoke. Mark the pole shoes so that they can be refitted in their original positions. When fitting the field coils, tighten the pole shoes with a wheel-operated screwdriver and secure the screws by caulking.

Examining and reconditioning: The commutator should be smooth and free from pits or burned spots. Slight irregularities may be rectified by lightly polishing the commutator with a piece of very fine sandpaper whilst rotating the commutator. A badly worn or burnt commutator may be turned down in a lathe, using a sharp tool and removing as little material as possible to obtain a smooth commutator face. After this operation, polish the commutator with very fine sandpaper. A moulded commutator should never be undercut; the slots, however, should be kept clear of carbon and copper deposits. If the commutator will not clean up at a minimum diameter of 1·43 in, renew the armature.

Check that the brushes can move freely in their holders. If not, they should be cleaned with a petrol-moistened cloth. Brushes which are cracked or worn to less than 9/32 in should be replaced. Test the brush spring tension using a suitable spring-balance; the tension should be above 13 oz. If the bearing bush in the commutator end-cover needs replacement, the bush can be removed by screwing a $\frac{5}{8}$ in tap squarely into the bush, after which the bush can be pulled out of its bore together with the tap.

Insert the felt ring and retainers into the bearing bore, and press in the new bearing bush until it is flush with the inner face of the end-cover.

NOTE: New bearing bushes must be soaked for 24 hours in SAE 30 engine oil.

The ball-bearing in the pulley end-cover can be removed as follows:

Drill out the rivets to release the end-plate. Remove the bearing from its housing. Remove the corrugated pressure washer and the felt ring.

Installation of the bearing assembly is a reversal of the removal procedure. Ideally the armature should be checked with the aid of a growler and voltage drop test equipment before reassembly.

Reassembly: Support the inner journal of the bearing to prevent damage when pressing the armature shaft through the bearing assembled in the pulley end-cover. Fit the armature and pulley end-cover to the yoke. Hold the brushes up in their holders by placing the brush springs on the sides of the brushes so that these are pinched in their holders. Fit the commutator end-cover so that the brushes are partially over the commutator and release the brushes by placing the springs in normal position. Secure the commutator end-cover with the two long through-bolts. Install the drive pulley with the Woodruff key.

Control box: The Lucas control box RB.340 is an electro-magnetically operated three-bobbin unit, operating on the current-voltage system of generator output regulation. See *Technical Data* for specifications.

Starter motor: The starter motor is mounted on the front right-hand side of the engine and is operated by a solenoid switch; the solenoid switch is controlled by the ignition key or alternatively by hand when the knob on the solenoid body is depressed. Should the starter motor drive become jammed in mesh with the starter ring gear, the drive pinion can be freed by rotating the armature with a spanner; the armature shaft is provided with a square end which can be reached after removing the thimble-type protective cover.

Dismantling: After removal from the vehicle, the starter motor can be dismantled as follows: First remove the starter drive assembly by depressing the retaining washer behind the circlip with the aid of a suitable hand-press, and remove the circlip. Remove the starter drive components. The pinion and barrel assembly and the threaded sleeve should never be replaced independently. Remove the commutator dust cover. Lift the brush springs to withdraw the brushes from the holders. Remove the two terminal nuts and the two long through-bolts. Withdraw the drive end-cover and the armature assembly from the yoke. If the field coils are to be replaced, mark the position of the pole shoes in relation to the yoke and remove the securing screws with a wheel-operated screwdriver. Unsolder the field coil tappings from the terminal posts. If necessary, the bearing bushes can be removed with a stepped mandrel of the same diameter as the armature shaft. The bronze bearing bushes are porous and should not be reamed-out after assembly. New bushes must be soaked for 24 hours in SAE 30 engine oil.

Inspection and reconditioning: The commutator should be perfectly smooth and free from pits or burned spots; if necessary, the commutator may be cleaned with very fine sandpaper wound round it whilst rotating the commutator. If this is unsatisfactory, the commutator may be machined in a high-speed lathe, using a very sharp tool and removing as little material as necessary to restore the polished surface.

NOTE: Under no circumstances should the insulation between the commutator segments be undercut.

Ensure that the carbon brushes move freely in their holders; if not, the sides of the brushes should be cleaned with a petrol-moistened rag and if necessary dressed with a smooth file. Check the brush spring tension using a spring balance; the tension should not be less than 30 oz. Check the length of the brushes; cracked or worn brushes should be replaced by cutting off the original flexible connector approximately ⅛ in short of the junction with the field coil; place the original flex joint within the loop of the connector of the new brush and solder the joint, taking care that no solder reaches the carbon. The brushes are preformed so that bedding-in on the commutator is unnecessary.

Reassembly: Reassembly is a reversal of the dismantling procedure.

Replacing lamp bulbs:

Headlamps (UK sealed-beam type): Remove the screw and prise off the rim. Remove the three crosshead unit retaining screws to release the unit. Withdraw the adaptor from the prongs on the rear of the unit. The two beam aiming screws need not be disturbed. Installation is a reversal of removal.

Side and direction-indicator lamp bulbs (front): After removal of the three screws, withdraw the lens and remove the bulb.

Rear lamp bulbs (stop/tail/direction-indicator): Access to these lamp bulbs can be gained by removing the screws securing the front edge of the trim in the luggage compartment; bend away the trim and withdraw the bulb-holders from their sockets.

Number-plate illumination bulbs: Take out the two screws attaching the covers and lenses; withdraw the bulbs.

Facia illumination and warning-light bulbs: Any of these light bulbs are accessible by withdrawing the instrument cluster from the facia. The warning-light cluster has an eight-bulb bulbholder panel, which is released by pulling off the connector block and undoing the screw in the back of the cluster housing.

Two-level signalling system relay: The purpose of the Lucas 11RA relay is to reduce the intensity of light emitted by the stop and rear direction-indicator lamps after dark. Basically it consists of three independent pairs of normally closed contacts, each having a resistor permanently connected in parallel with it, plus a fourth, current compensating resistor, to maintain the correct frequency of operation of the flasher unit, and a shunt-wound operating coil energised from the side and tail-lamp switch. This relay requires no attention in service. In the event of failure, the unit must be replaced complete.

Bulb chart:

	Watts
Headlamps, right-hand drive (sealed beam):	60/45
left-hand drive (sealed beam):	50/40
Side lamps:	6
Direction-indicator lamps, front:	21
Direction-indicator lamps, rear:	21
Stop/tail lamps:	21/6
Number plate illumination:	5
Interior roof lamp:	6
Instrument illumination:	2·2
Warning light cluster:	1·5

Key to wiring diagrams, Figs. 33 *and* 34

A	Ammeter	IL	Interior light
B	Battery	ILS	Interior light switch
CO	Coil	IN	Instrument light
CW	Choke warning light	INR	Instrument light rheostat
CWS	Choke warning light switch	IS/STS	Ignition/starter switch
DF	Direction indicator flasher	IW	Ignition/generator warning light
DI.L.F.	Direction indicator, left front	LL	Numberplate lamp
DI.L.R.	Direction indicator, left rear	LU	Luggage compartment lamp
DI.R.F.	Direction indicator, right front	LUS	Luggage compartment lamp switch
DI.R.R.	Direction indicator, right rear	LS	Light switch
DIS	Distributor	OL	Oil pressure warning light
DS	Direction indicator switch	OP	Oil pressure warning light switch
DSW	Door switch	PBL	Parking brake warning light
DW.L	Direction indicator warning light, left	PBS	Parking brake warning light switch
		R.L	Rear lamp, left
DW.R	Direction indicator warning light, right	R.R	Rear lamp, right
		RL	Relay
FG	Fuel gauge	RES	Resistor
FGU	Fuel gauge tank unit	SL.L	Sidelamp, left
FU	Fuses	SL.R	Sidelamp, right
FW	Fuel reserve warning light	SM	Starter motor
GEN	Generator	SSO	Starter motor solenoid
GVR	Gauge voltage regulator	SSW	Stoplamp switch
H	Horn	STL.L	Stoplamp, left
HB	Horn contact	STL.R	Stoplamp, right
HL.L	Headlamp, left	TG	Water temperature gauge
HL.R	Headlamp, right	TGS	Water temperature gauge transmitter
HLW	Mainbeam warning light	VR	Voltage regulator
HM	Heater motor	WI	Windscreen wiper
HS	Heater motor switch	WIS	Windscreen wiper switch

Key to wire colours, Figs. 33 *and* 34

2	Blue/red				
4	Blue/white	20	Green/blue	41	Red
9	White	21	Green/white	44	Red/white
10	White/red	22	Green/purple	45	Red/green
12	White/blue	23	Green/brown	49	Purple
13	White/green	24	Green/black	53	Purple/white
15	White/brown	29	Yellow/green	56	Purple/black
16	White/black	33	Brown	57	Black
17	Green	34	Brown/red	106	Light green/blue
18	Green/red	35	Brown/yellow	107	Light green/purple
19	Green/yellow	37	Brown/white	108	Light green/brown

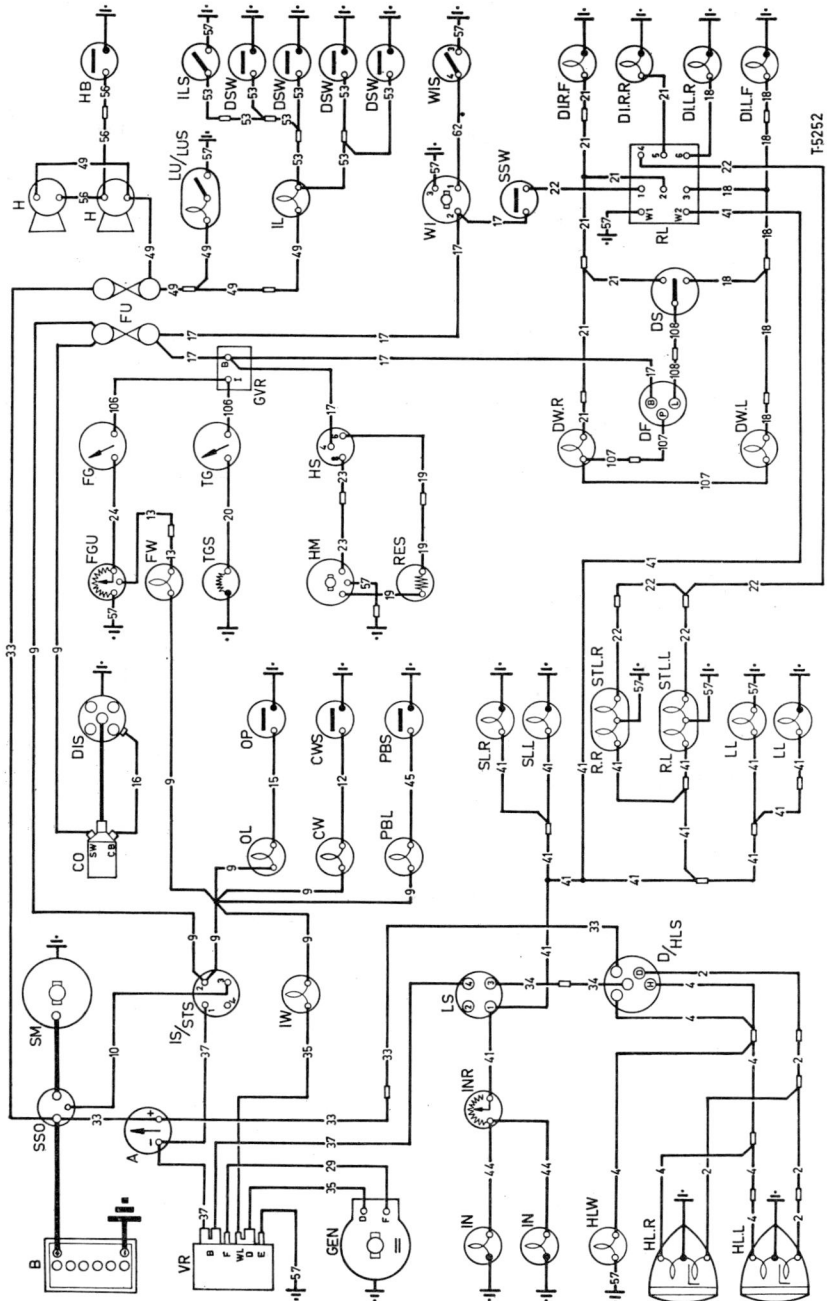

Fig. 33. Wiring diagram

E

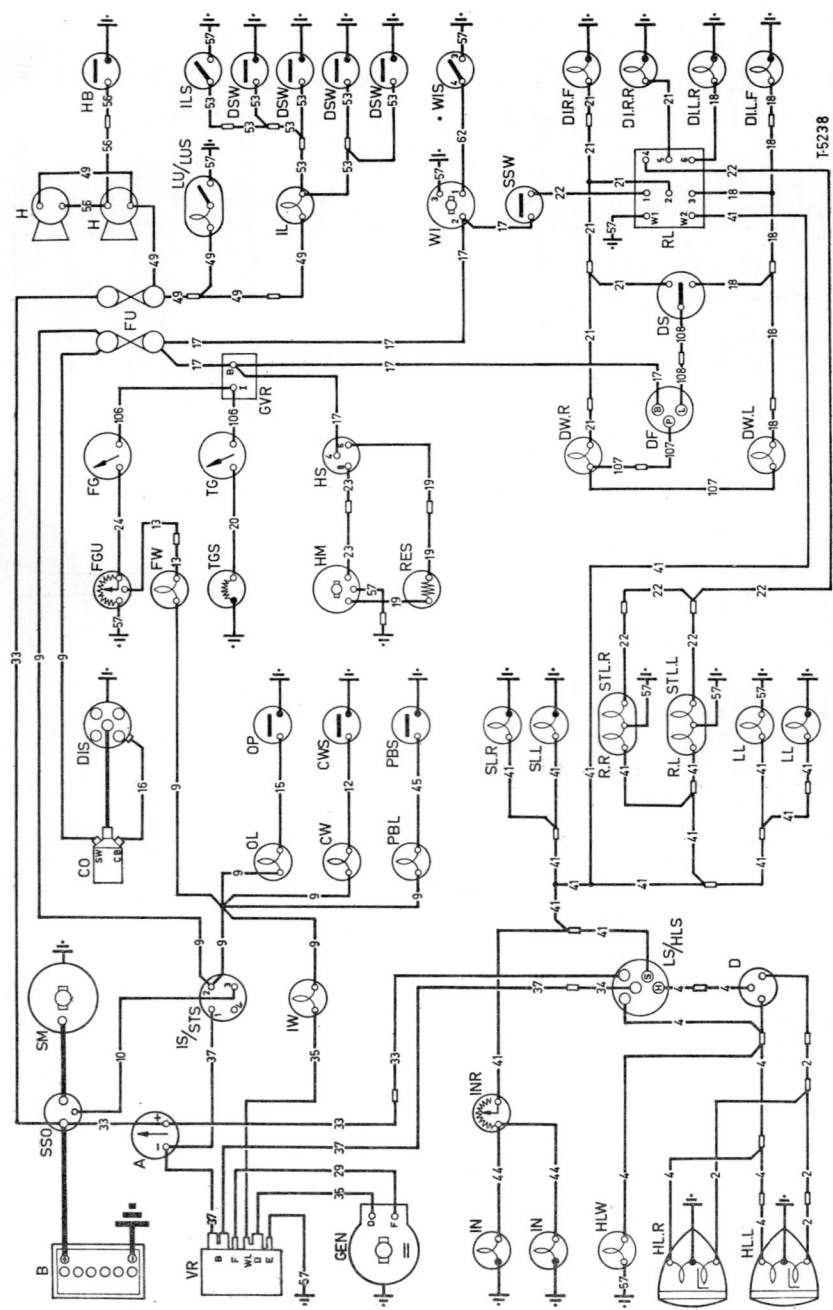

Fig. 34. Wiring diagram, cars for North American market

Technical Data

ENGINE:

NOTE: For general engine data see page 8; for 1300 TC see page 66

Valves:

Valve head diameter, inlet:	1·304–1·308 in
Valve stem diameter, inlet:	0·3107–0·3112 in
Valve head diameter, exhaust:	1·168–1·172 in
Valve stem diameter, exhaust:	0·310–0·3105 in
Valve stem to guide clearance, inlet	0·0023–0·008 in
exhaust:	0·0015–0·003 in
Valve clearance (cold):	0·010 in

Valve seats:

	Insert dimensions		Bore in cylinder head	
	external dia	width	diameter	depth
Exhaust:	1·252–1·253 in	0·248–0·250 in	1·249–1·25 in	0·248–0·250 in
Inlet:	1·3785–1·3795 in	0·216–0·219 in	1·375–1·376 in	0·216–0·219 in

Valve guides:

Length:	2·0625 in
Bore:	0·312–0·313 in
Outer diameter:	0·501–0·502 in
Amount of protrusion above cylinder head:	0·749–0·751 in

Valve springs:

Length:	1·36 in
Tension:	27–30 lb
Number of coils:	7¼

Valve tappets:

Tappet diameter:	0·7996–0·8000 in
Tappet bore in crankcase:	0·8002–0·8009 in

Valve timing: see procedure on page 22.

Valve rockers and valve rocker shaft:

Valve rocker bore:	0·562–0·563 in
Rocker shaft diameter:	0·5607–0·5612 in

Pistons:

	Grading dimensions for standard-size cylinders	
	F	G
Bore:	2·900–2·8995 in	2·9005–2·9001 in
Automotive Engineering Co. Ltd.:		
Piston, diameter at top:	2·880–2·8752 in	2·880–2·8752 in
Piston, diameter at bottom:	2·8981–2·8976 in	2·8987–2·8982 in
British Piston Ring Co. Ltd.:		
Piston, diameter at top:	2·880–2·8752 in	2·880–2·8752 in
Piston, diameter at bottom:	2·8981–2·8976 in	2·8987–2·8982 in
Hepworth:		
Piston, diameter at top:	2·87993–2·8752 in	2·87993–2·8752 in
Piston, diameter at bottom:	2·8981–2·8976 in	2·8987–2·8983 in

Piston rings:

Compression ring width:	0·0620–0·0625 in
Compression ring clearance in groove:	0·0015–0·0035 in
Oil control ring width:	0·1553–0·1563 in
Oil control ring clearance in groove:	0·0015–0·0035 in
Piston ring gaps (all rings) when fitted:	0·012–0·022 in

Piston ring grooves:

Compression rings, grooves, width:	0·0640–0·0650 in
Oil control ring grooves, width:	0·1578–0·1588 in

Piston pins:

Diameter ('High' grade):	0·8123–0·81250 in

Connecting rods and bearings:

Big-end bearing, internal diameter:	1·626–1·627 in
Big-end bearing end-float:	0·0025–0·0086 in
Small-end bore:	0·8110–0·8115 in
Maximum connecting rod bend or twist:	0·0015 in
Available undersize big-end bearing shells:	0·010 in, 0·020 in, 0·030 in

Crankshaft and main bearings:

Main bearing journal diameter:	2·0005–2·001 in
Rear bearing journal width:	1·2975–1·2995 in
Crankpin diameter:	1·625–1·6255 in
Main bearings inside diameter:	2·0020–2·0025 in
Ground bore for main bearings in crankcase:	2·146–2·1465 in
Thickness of thrust washers, standard:	0·091–0·093 in
Available oversize thrust washers:	0·096–0·098 in
Available undersize main bearing shells:	0·010 in, 0·020 in, 0·030 in, 0·040 in

Camshaft:

Bearing journal diameter:	1·9649–1·9654 in
Bearing ground bore in crankcase:	1·9680–1·9695 in
Camshaft end-float:	0·0035–0·0085 in

Oil pump:

Make and type:	Hobourn-Eaton, eccentric rotor
Depth of rotor:	0·9985–0·9995 in
Housing depth:	1·001–1·002 in
Maximum permissible clearance between outer rotor and body:	0·0075 in
Maximum permissible clearance between both rotors:	0·010 in
Maximum wear of pump cover:	0·004 in

Oil pressure relief valve spring:

Free length:	1·53 in minimum
Fitted length:	1·25 in
Tension when fitted:	14·5 lb
Normal oil pressure at 2000 rpm (engine):	60 lb/sq in

Fuel pump:

Make and type:	AC mechanical
Pump pressure:	2 lb/sq in approx.

Ignition system:

Distributor, make and type:	Lucas 25 D4 with centrifugal and vacuum advance
Firing order:	1–3–4–2
Dwell angle:	60° ± 3°
Rotation (as seen from top):	counter-clockwise
Contact breaker points gap:	0·014–0·016 in
Ignition timing:	9° BTDC

Distributor drive gear:

End-float:	0·003–0·007 in
Spindle diameter:	0·498–0·4985 in
Bush bore:	0·5005–0·501 in

Centrifugal advance characteristics (*high compression*):
Set at 0° at less than 100 rpm
Up to 1500 distributor rpm advance should be 6° to 8°
Advance at decelerating speeds (*distributor rpm and angle*):

rpm	angle
1100	6°–8°
850	$3\frac{1}{2}°$–$5\frac{1}{2}°$
550	$\frac{1}{2}°$–$2\frac{1}{2}°$
400	0°–1°

No advance below 300 rpm
Vacuum advance characteristics (*decelerating with a closed throttle*):

Vacuum in Hg	Advance degrees (distr.)
15	7°–9°
11	$6\frac{1}{2}°$–$8\frac{1}{2}°$
$6\frac{1}{2}$	1°–3°
4	0°–$\frac{1}{2}°$

No advance below 3 in Hg

Spark plugs: Champion N–9Y, $\frac{3}{4}$ in reach, extended nose 14 mm, gap 0·025 in

Cooling system:

Type: pressurised radiator with 'no-loss' expansion tank, water pump, thermostat and fan

Thermostat opens at: 79·5° to 83·5°C; fully open at 93·5° to 96°C

Relief valve in radiator cap opens at: 7 lb/sq in

TRANSMISSION

Clutch:

Make and type: Borg and Beck, 6½ in diameter, diaphragm type

Operation: hydraulic

Adjustment: release lever hinge plate

Gearbox:

Cluster gear end-float: 0·003–0·013 in

Outside diameter of cluster gear bushes: 0·7821–0·7835 in

Inside diameter of cluster gear bushes: 0·6581–0·6605 in

Idler gear end-float: 0·001–0·003 in

Outside diameter of reverse idler bush: 0·7830–0·7840 in

Inside diameter of reverse idler bush: 0·6883–0·6890 in

Input gear end-float: 0·026–0·028 in

First- and third-gear end-floats: 0·0030–0·01 in

Second-gear end-float: 0·0030–0·0095 in

Top-gear end-float: 0·006–0·011 in

Synchroniser release loads,

     first- and second-gear synchroniser unit: 8–12 lb

     Third- and top-gear synchroniser unit: 8–12 lb

Final drive/Differential:

Type: hypoid bevel gears

Crownwheel:

Number of teeth: 37

Backlash: 0·004–0·006 in

Mainshaft/Pinion:

Number of teeth: 9

Journal diameter for rear pinion bearing: 1·1880–1·1885 in

Journal diameter for front pinion bearing: 1·3135–1·3140 in

Pinion bearing pre-load: 12–20 lb ft

Differential assembly:

Sun gear spigot diameter: 1·3110–1·3118 in

Planet gear internal diameter: 0·5000–0·5015 in

Backlash between planet and sun gears: 0·002–0·004 in

Clearance between thrust block and sun gears: 0·002–0·004 in

Axle-shaft and differential carriers:

Axle-shaft carrier bush outside diameter: 1·1910–1·925 in

Axle-shaft carrier bush inside diameter: 1·0625–1·0637 in

Maximum permissible carrier flange run-out: 0·003 in

CHASSIS

Suspension:

Wheelbase: 8 ft ⅝ in

Ground clearance: 5½ in

Front springs:

Material diameter: 0·435 ± 0·002 in

Mean coil diameter: 3·130 ± 0·020 in

Number of effective coils: 10¼

Free length: 12·30 in

Fitted length at 850 lb load: 7·12 ± 0·09 in

Maximum permissible 'out of square' per foot length: 0·19 in

F

Front wheel alignment:

Caster:	$+2° \pm 1°$
Camber:	$0° \pm 1°$
Steering axis inclination:	$11°$
Toe-out:	0 to $\frac{1}{16}$ in
Track:	4ft 5in
Toe-out on turns (outside wheel 20°):	inside wheel 21°
(outside wheel 35° 30'):	inside wheel 44° 30' maximum

Rear springs:

Material diameter:	$0\cdot460 \pm 0\cdot002$ in
Mean coil diameter:	$3\cdot625 \pm 0\cdot020$ in
Number of effective coils:	$6\frac{3}{4}$
Free length:	$11\cdot76$ in
Fitted length at 890lb load:	$7\cdot31 \pm 0\cdot09$ in
Maximum permissible 'out of square' per foot length:	$0\cdot19$ in

Rear wheel alignment:

Caster:	$+2° \pm 1°$
Camber:	$+1\frac{1}{4}° \pm 1°$
Toe-out:	0 to $\frac{1}{16}$ in
Track:	4ft $4\frac{5}{8}$ in

Steering gear:

Type:	rack and pinion
Steering wheel turns (lock to lock):	$3\frac{1}{4}$ turns
Steering wheel diameter:	16in
Turning circle:	29ft
Maximum back lock:	$44\frac{1}{2}°$
Maximum front lock:	$35\frac{1}{2}°$
Fitted track-rod length (taken between ball-joint centre lines):	$9\cdot656$ in

Brakes:

Disc brakes front: (Girling)

Brake disc diameter:	$8\frac{3}{4}$ in
Minimum permissible brake disc thickness:	$0\cdot335$ in
Maximum permissible brake disc run-out:	$0\cdot002$–$0\cdot004$ in
Minimum permissible brake-pad lining thickness:	$\frac{1}{8}$ in

Drum brakes rear: (Lockheed)

Brake drum diameter:	8in
Brake drum width:	$1\frac{1}{4}$ in

Wheels and tyres:

Rim type and size:	steel, 4J x 13
Maximum permissible axial run-out:	3/32in
Maximum permissible radial run-out:	3/32in
Tyre size and pressures:	see page 11

ELECTRICAL EQUIPMENT

Type and earthing:	12 volts, negative (—) connected to earth

Battery:

Type:	6–VTAZ.9BR
Capacity:	34 Ah at 10-hr rate, 39 Ah at 20-hr rate
Initial charging current:	4 amperes
Recharging current:	5 amperes

Generator:

	Lucas C40–1
Field coil resistance:	6 Ohms
Maximum output at $13\cdot5$ volts:	22 amps at 2250rpm
Maximum permissible brush tension:	30oz
Minimum permissible brush length:	9/32in
Voltage regulator:	Lucas RB340
Cut-in voltage:	$12\cdot6$–$13\cdot4$ volts
Cut-out voltage:	$9\cdot3$–$11\cdot2$ volts

Swamp resistor (measured on unit between centre and base):		13·25 to 14·25 Ohms
Contact resistor:		55–65 Ohms
No-load voltage	10°C (50°F):	14·9–15·5 V
regulator settings	20°C (68°F):	14·7–15·3 V
	30°C (86°F):	14·5–15·1 V
	40°C (104°F):	14·3–14·9 V
Current regulator setting:		21–23 A
Starter motor:		Lucas M.35 G–1, four-pole, four-brush. series wound
Minimum permissible brush tension (new):		30–34 oz
Minimum permissible brush length:		5/16 in
Locking torque:		7·7 lb ft at 7·5–7·1 volts
Stall torque current:		370 amp
Torque at 1000 rpm:		4·5 lb ft at 9·1–8·7 volts, 215–235 amp

TIGHTENING TORQUES (in lb ft)

Engine:

Cylinder-head stud-nuts:	42–46
Manifolds to cylinder head:	
inlet 1·34 in stud nut:	24–26
1·84 in stud nut:	24–26
exhaust 1·31 in stud nut:	12–14
Rockershaft supports to cylinder head:	28–30
Rocker cover attachment:	1½
Water pump to cylinder head:	18–20
Camshaft sprocket attachment nut:	24–26
Camshaft locating plate to cylinder block:	18–20
Engine front mounting plate to cylinder block:	18–20
Crankshaft oil-seal cover to cylinder block:	18–20
Crankshaft sealing block to cylinder block:	12–14
Connecting-rod bolts:	38–42
Main bearing cap-bolts:	55–60
Flywheel to crankshaft bolts:	42–46
Flywheel/clutch attachment:	18–20
Sparking plug:	14–16
Starter ring assembly attachment:	90–100
Engine to transmission case,	
8·69 in bolts:	28–30
setscrews:	18–20
2⅜ in bolts:	18–20
3 in bolts:	18–20

Transmission:

Crownwheel attachment:	40–45
Pinion/mainshaft speedometer gear attachment:	60–65
Hinge plate to transmission case:	18–20
Internal gear selector fork and reverse idler gear attachment:	8–10
Idler gear shaft attachment—to give end-play as in specification.	
Idler gear attachment:	8–10
Inner axle carriers to transmission case:	18–20

Rotoflex coupling to drive shaft:	65–70
Hypoid pinion pre-load nut:	100–110
Front cover to transmission case:	18–20

Front Suspension:

Ball-joint and tie-rod lever to vertical link:	55–60
Brake disc to hub:	18–20
Disc brake caliper to vertical link:	45–50
Front strut to top wishbone:	55–60
Front strut top mounting to body:	18–20
Lower shock-absorber mounting to plate:	55–60
Front hub to drive shaft:	55–60
Outer drive flange to drive shaft:	100–110
Lower ball-pin attachment:	38–42
Upper ball-pin attachment:	55–65
Upper ball-pin housing and damper to wishbone:	28–30
Top wishbone to fulcrum shaft:	22–24
Lower wishbone to mounting bracket:	28–30
Lower strut to wishbone:	55–60
Lower strut to sub-frame:	34–36
Road wheel securing nuts:	38–42

Rear suspension:

Rear hub to stub axle:	55–60
Trailing arm to fulcrum bracket:	55–60
Fulcrum bracket to cross-member:	28–30
Shock-absorber to mounting strap:	55–60
Shock-absorber mounting strap to trailing arm:	28–30
Road wheel securing nuts:	38–42

Steering gear:

Ball-joint assembly to tie-rod	26–28
Ball ends inner attachment:	40–45
Rack assembly attachment to front sub-frame:	12–14
Universal joint attachment:	18–20
Steering wheel attachment:	28–30

TRIUMPH 1300 TC   from 1967

The Triumph 1300 TC (twin-carburettor) model was first announced on 3 October 1967. It is an additional model, basically similar to the normal version but with increased top speed and acceleration. This has been achieved by increasing the compression ratio of the 1296-cc engine and fitting twin SU carburettors as well as a modified camshaft and crankshaft. The new 75-bhp engine is basically similar to that of the current Triumph Spitfire. The brake system is servo-assisted. For further details see *Technical and Adjustment Data*.

IDENTIFICATION

The 1300 TC can externally be identified only by "TC" badges on the front wings and at the rear. Otherwise the body specification is identical to that of the normal 1300. The car commission number (car serial number) is prefixed "RF" and the starting serial number is RF 1 DL.

PRICES (UK)

	Basic	*Purchase Tax*	*Total*
October 1967	£710	£164 8 6	£874 8 6

PERFORMANCE FIGURES (manufacturer's data)

Acceleration:
through gears,   0–50 mph 11.5 sec   0–60 mph 16.0 sec
top gear,   20–40 mph 12.5 sec   30–50 mph 12.5 sec   40–60 mph 13.5 sec
Maximum speed: 90 mph (equivalent to 5800 engine rpm).
Braking: maximum retardation 0.92 (equivalent to stopping from 30 mph in 32.5 ft).

TECHNICAL AND ADJUSTMENT DATA

NOTE: Service and repair operations are basically the same as described for the normal 1300 model. The following are the main differences between the two models.

ENGINE

Engine performance data:
Compression ratio: 9.0:1
Maximum bhp (net) at rpm: 75 at 6000
Maximum bmep at rpm: 144 lb/sq in at 4000
Maximum torque (net) at rpm: 75 lb ft at 4000
Mean piston speed at maximum bhp: 2990 ft/min

Crankcase ventilation: There is a positive (closed circuit) crankcase ventilation system incorporating a breather or emission valve unit between the inlet manifold and the valve rocker cover. Every 6000 miles this valve should be disassembled and the various components (including the diaphragm and spring) cleaned by swilling them in methylated spirit (denatured alcohol). Ensure that the breather pipe is clean and serviceable. After cleaning the valve, remove the oil filler cap from the rocker cover. Check the breather hole is clear and the joint washer serviceable.

Manifolds: The cast aluminium inlet manifold is water-heated. The exhaust manifold is a fabricated steel four-branch unit.

Carburettors: Twin SU model HS2. Needle size BO. An exploded view of a typical SU HS2 carburettor is shown in Fig. 37.

Fig. 35. Triumph 1300 TC Saloon, three-quarter rear view

Fig. 36. Triumph 1300 TC, under-bonnet view

Dampers

Every 6000 miles check the oil level in the dashpots or damper reservoirs and top up with the current grade of engine oil if necessary. The oil level is correct when, using the damper piston stem as a dipstick, its threaded hexagon plug is $\frac{1}{4}$ in above the dashpot when resistance is felt.

Adjustment and synchronisation of two carburettors:

Make sure that the vacuum chambers and pistons on both carburettors are clean, needles properly fitted and the jets correctly centred. Check the dampers for correct oil level and top-up if necessary, then proceed as follows:

(1) Remove air-cleaner, and slacken the clamping bolt on the throttle interconnecting rod to enable each throttle to be set independently. Ensure that the idle-adjustment screws are holding the throttles partly open and that the jet adjustment nuts are not screwed all the way up. (An average setting to start with is obtained by turning the idle-adjustment screws down one full turn from the fully closed position, and the jet-adjusting nuts one-and-a-half turns down from the top position.)

(2) Make sure the jet seats against the adjusting nut; if necessary, re-adjust or disconnect the choke cable.

(3) Warm-up the engine, set throttles to give an idling speed of about 500 rpm.

(4) Listen to the hiss of air at each carburettor air-intake (the use of a piece of tubing of about $\frac{3}{8}$ in diameter, one end held to the ear and the other to each air-intake in turn will make it easier to compare the sound of both carburettors).

(5) Adjust both idle-screws until the hiss is equal on both units and the idle speed is approximately 500 rpm.

(6) Now turn off the ignition and with a downward pressure on the rear throttle arm, tighten the throttle connector-rod clamping screw.

(7) Start the engine. While the engine is idling at approximately 500 rpm, check the mixture of each carburettor in turn by lifting the piston approximately $\frac{1}{32}$ in by means of the built-in piston lifting pin.

NOTE: Do not lift the piston with a finger, since a finger forms a too large obstruction of the air-intake; it will alter the mixture and lead to false conclusions.

(8) If, when the piston is lifted, the engine speed increases, the mixture is too rich and the jet adjusting nut must be screwed up one sixth of a turn. If the speed decreases, the mixture is too lean and the nut should be turned down.

(9) Continue adjusting each carburettor until, when either piston is lifted, no increase, or a very slight increase followed by a decrease in speed, is noticed. The mixture is then correct and the engine should run evenly.

(10) Reconnect and adjust the choke cable. Adjust the "fast-idle" adjustment screw on the connecting linkage between choke lever and throttle until the tip of the screw is just clear of the cam; the clearance should be about $\frac{1}{64}$ in.

(11) Refit the air-cleaner. Recheck idle speed and mixture.

Checking the float setting

With the float chamber lid and float assembly removed and inverted (float lever resting on needle valve) the distance between float lever and lower lid face should be 0.125 in. If necessary bend lever to obtain this setting.

Centring the jets

When assembling the carburettor, it is imperative to make sure that the jet and needle are correctly centred. This is done by screwing the adjustment nut all the way up; then lift the piston and needle assembly and listen for it to fall freely with

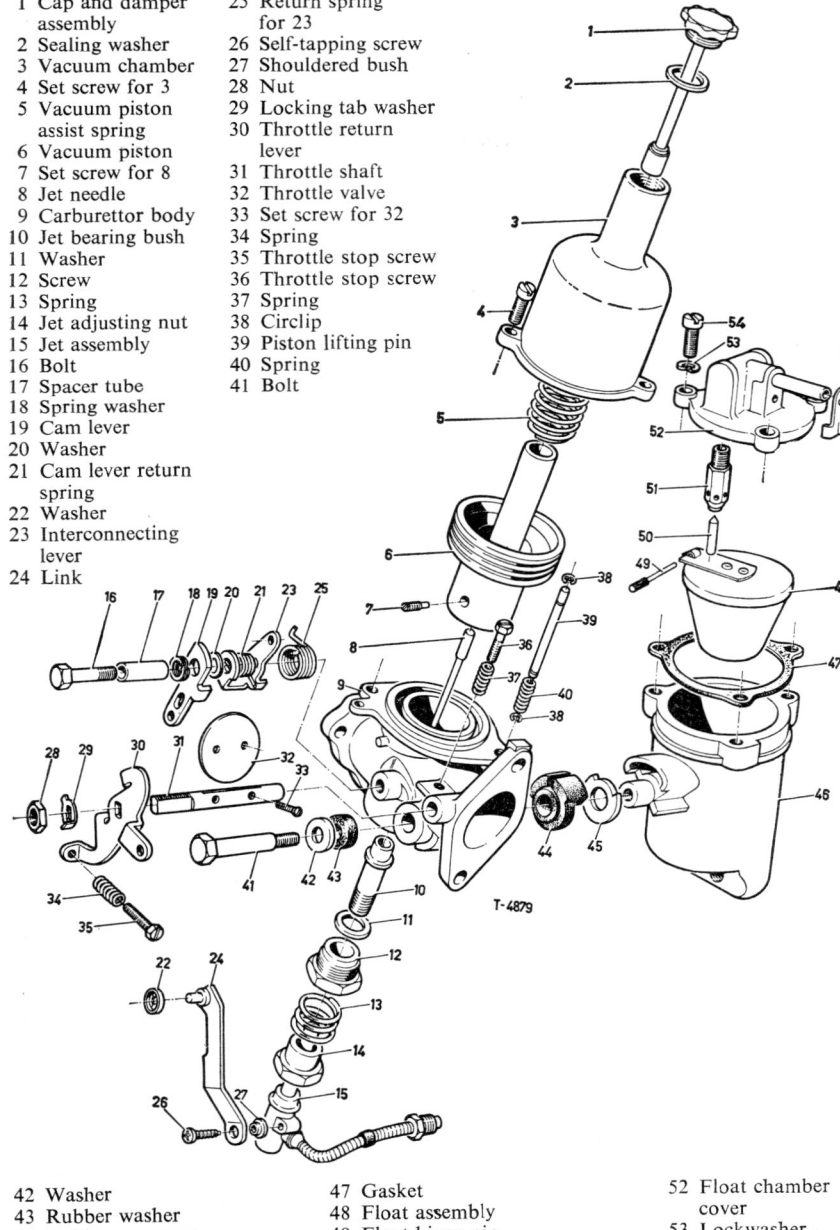

 1 Cap and damper
   assembly
 2 Sealing washer
 3 Vacuum chamber
 4 Set screw for 3
 5 Vacuum piston
   assist spring
 6 Vacuum piston
 7 Set screw for 8
 8 Jet needle
 9 Carburettor body
10 Jet bearing bush
11 Washer
12 Screw
13 Spring
14 Jet adjusting nut
15 Jet assembly
16 Bolt
17 Spacer tube
18 Spring washer
19 Cam lever
20 Washer
21 Cam lever return
   spring
22 Washer
23 Interconnecting
   lever
24 Link

25 Return spring
   for 23
26 Self-tapping screw
27 Shouldered bush
28 Nut
29 Locking tab washer
30 Throttle return
   lever
31 Throttle shaft
32 Throttle valve
33 Set screw for 32
34 Spring
35 Throttle stop screw
36 Throttle stop screw
37 Spring
38 Circlip
39 Piston lifting pin
40 Spring
41 Bolt

42 Washer
43 Rubber washer
44 Rubber grommet
45 Support washer
46 Float chamber

47 Gasket
48 Float assembly
49 Float hinge pin
50 Float valve needle
51 Float valve seat

52 Float chamber
   cover
53 Lockwasher
54 Set screw for 52
55 Baffle plate

T-4879

Fig. 37. SU HS2 carburettor (typical), exploded view

an audible "click." If no click is heard, the needle is fouling the jet, which will have to be re-centred. This is done by loosening and retightening the jet retainer. Re-check whether the piston will now fall with an audible "click"; if necessary, repeat loosening and retightening the jet retainer until the jet is centred correctly.

Maintenance

In addition to the topping up of the damper oil reservoirs and the tuning described earlier, the maintenance requirements of the SU carburettor are confined to periodically cleaning the suction chambers and pistons (once a year) and the float chambers. When reassembling the suction chambers and pistons these should be entirely clean and dry, except for a few spots of clean engine oil on the piston rods.

Air Cleaner: The air cleaner contains two replaceable paper elements which should be cleaned every 6000 miles, renewed every 12000 miles. Under extremely dusty conditions they should be cleaned at shorter intervals. Use a soft brush or compressed air to remove dust and other foreign matter from the folds of the elements.

Ignition system: The timing mark is scribed on the starter ring carrier, aligned with left-hand corner of timing case pointer (when viewed from the front). This mark represents 4° BTDC which is the correct static ignition timing.

CHASSIS

Brake system: The Girling brake system comprises discs at front, drums at rear, with vacuum servo assistance. The brake dimensions are as follows:
  Lining area (sq in), front: 14.8, rear: 38, total: 52.
  Swept area (sq in), front: 145, rear: 63, total: 208.

Vacuum servo unit: The Girling brake servo unit is mounted alongside the dynamo. It serves to reduce brake-pedal pressure and is installed in the hydraulic system so that the master cylinder outlet is connected to the servo inlet port and the servo outlet port is connected to the wheel cylinders. The vacuum servo is interconnected with the engine inlet manifold, from which it obtains its operating vacuum; this means that the vacuum servo unit operates only when the engine is running. If for some reason the engine should stall, the unit becomes inoperative due to the lack of vacuum, thus rendering the brake system a conventional hydraulic brake system without servo assistance.

Removal of the servo unit

Disconnect the vacuum hose from the servo, discarding the two sealing washers as they must be renewed. Disconnect the hydraulic pipes from the inlet and outlet ports, taking care to catch the escaping brake fluid. Remove the bolts and washers securing the servo unit to the mounting bracket and lift the unit from the car. Installation is a direct reversal of the removal procedure. However, the hydraulic system must be bled to remove all air before the engine is started, as once vacuum is available operation of the brake pedal seals the low and high pressure systems of the servo from each other, making adequate bleeding impossible.

NOTE: **Servicing or reconditioning the vacuum servo unit is not recommended. If the unit does not function satisfactorily it is best to replace the complete assembly.**

Regular maintenance

The brake servo air filter has a replaceable element of moulded cellular construction which should be renewed whenever replacement brake shoes are fitted or at least every 12000 miles. The filter unit is held in place by a single central screw. Renew the element and the rubber pad underneath it and clean the base plate.

GENERAL FAULT FINDING CHART
FOR PETROL ENGINES

Some items in this chart are not applicable to *every* make of petrol engine

Engine will not start

A. Starter does not crank engine

Battery run down	*Recharge; replace if defective*
Battery posts and terminals loose or corroded	*Clean and tighten. If badly corroded, soak with water to facilitate removal and avoid damage to the battery posts*
Faulty starter switch or solenoid, if fitted; broken battery cable or loose connection	*Check wires and cables; check solenoid and switch, replace if defective*
Starter motor defective	*Repair or replace*
Starter drive stuck (starter will run, but does not crank engine)	*Clean and if necessary repair or replace*
Starter drive pinion jammed with starter ring gear	*Free by rotating squared end of starter spindle with a spanner*

B. Starter cranks engine slowly

Battery partly run down	*Recharge; replace if defective*
Loose or corroded connections	*Clean and tighten*
Faulty starter switch or solenoid; partly broken cable or loose connection	*Check wires and cables: check solenoid and switch, replace if necessary*
Starter motor defective	*Repair or replace*

C. Starter cranks engine, but engine will not start

Trouble in ignition system:

No spark at plugs:

Moisture on spark plugs, ignition distributor, coil and wires (this trouble often occurs after parking overnight in foggy or rainy weather)	*Clean and dry. Avoid recurrence by coating wires, distributor rotor, cap, coil and spark plug insulators with moisture-proof lacquer*
Spark plugs flooded, due to excessive use of choke	*Start engine on full throttle, If this does not help, clean plugs. With plugs removed, turn over the crankshaft a few times to blow the accumulated fuel from the cylinders*

Spark plugs oiled-up	*Clean: if necessary replace*
Spark plug insulator cracked	*Replace*
Spark plug gap too wide or too close	*Reset gap*
No spark at distributor:	
Loose, broken or shorted low-tension lead between coil and/or inside distributor	*Check and tighten: also check internal leads in distributor. These leads sometimes break inside their insulation, and the break is not always visible. Pull carefully on one end: a broken lead will stretch*
Cracked rotor or distributor cap	*Replace*
Contact breaker points dirty, worn or maladjusted	*Clean and adjust: if necessary replace*
Carbon brush in distributor cap not making contact	*Free: if necessary replace*
Faulty condenser	*Replace*
No spark at coil:	
High-tension lead loose or broken	*Replace*
Broken or loose low-tension leads or faulty ignition switch	*Check wiring, repair or replace: check switch, replace if defective*

D. Starter cranks engine, but engine will not start

Trouble in fuel system:	
No petrol in carburettor:	
Empty fuel tank	*Fill up. If necessary, check and repair or replace fuel gauge*
Obstructed or damaged fuel pipe	*Clean: if necessary repair or replace*
Air leak in petrol line	*Check and repair or replace. Pay special attention to flexible fuel line (if fitted). If flexible fuel line is porous, a temporary 'get-you-home' repair can often be made by securely wrapping the line with friction tape or rubbing with hard soap*
Fuel filter clogged	*Clean and refit with new gasket. Always carry a spare gasket and a glass filter bowl, if so equipped*

Fuel pump defective	*Repair or replace. If electric pump does not function, lightly tap pump housing until ticking resumes*
Petrol in carburettor:	
Jets clogged	*Clean: blow out with air (never use wire to clean jets)*
Float needle stuck	*Clean or replace*
Carburettor flooded	*Clean float needle valve: if necessary replace. If this trouble persists: check fuel pump pressure*
Choke control faulty	*Repair or replace*
Air leak at inlet manifold or carburettor base	*Check nuts and bolts for tightness: if necessary replace gaskets*
Water or dirt in carburettor	*Clean. If this trouble persists, check rubber hose in fuel tank filler neck for damage or looseness, causing water to enter tank*

NOTE: *If the ignition system and carburettor are in order, yet the engine will not start, check timing.*

Engine starts but does not run properly

E. Engine misfires	
Ignition trouble:	
Spark plug or coil leads loose or damaged	*Tighten: replace if necessary*
Incorrect spark plug gap	*Regap*
Cracked spark plug insulator	*Replace faulty spark plug*
Spark plug oiled-up	*Clean, if necessary replace with spark plug of correct type. If trouble persists, check for mechanical trouble*
Cracked distributor cap	*Replace*
Loose connection in primary circuit	*Check and repair. Also check, and if necessary replace, ignition switch. In rare cases the ammeter has been found to be the cause of this trouble, due to faulty internal connection*
Distributor otherwise faulty	*See* C
Trouble in fuel system:	*See* D

Mechanical trouble:

Incorrect valve clearance	*Adjust*
Valve sticking	*Try to free by pouring a gum solvent of good quality into carburettor air intake: if not successful, dismantle and repair*
Valve spring broken	*Replace. Usually the valve concerned will have to be ground*
Worn piston, piston rings and cylinder or burnt valve; Cylinder-head gasket blown	*Test compression: if too low, dismantle for repairs*

F. Engine starts and stops

Trouble in ignition or fuel system:	*See* **C** *and* **D**
Obstructed exhaust system	*Check and repair or replace*

G. Engine runs on wide throttle only

Idle jet clogged or mixture improperly adjusted	*Clean idle jet and/or idle air bleed; adjust*
Valve sticking or burnt; valve spring broken; other mechanical trouble	*Check and repair. Pay special attention to heat riser, if so equipped, since a burnt heat riser will cause exhaust gas to enter intake manifold. This will sometimes cause backfiring in carburettor*

H. Lack of power

Ignition too far retarded or other ignition trouble	*Check and correct (see* **C***)*
Obstructed exhaust system	*Dented exhaust pipe and/or muffler Dislocated baffle plate in muffler Replace*
Trouble in fuel system	*Check and correct (see* **D***)*
Loss of compression	*Test compression: if found to be too low, check valve clearance. If valve clearance is properly adjusted and compression us still low, check for other mechanical trouble, such as burnt valve and/or worn pistons, rings and cylinders*
Dragging brakes	*Check and correct. Essentially this is not an engine trouble*

I. Engine runs roughly

Ignition timing incorrect	*Check and correct. Pay attention to possibly stuck advance mechanism, because the fixed advance may be correctly adjusted, yet the timing while running will be incorrect if the automatic advance is stuck*
Lean or rich mixture	*Check carburettor and fuel system (see D)*
Improperly adjusted valve clearance	*Check and correct*

J. Engine knocks

Ignition too far advanced	*Check and correct. Attend to possibly stuck advance mechanism (see I)*
Excessive carbon deposit	*Decarbonise*
Loose bearings or pistons or other mechanical cause	*Check and repair*

K. Engine overheats

Cooling system:	
Lack of water	*Top-up and check for leaks*
Fan belt loose or broken	*Check and adjust or replace*
Radiator clogged by insects	*Clean*
Cooling system clogged internally	*Clean with a cooling system cleaner of a reputable make and flush out according to maker's instructions. Inspect radiator hoses and replace if in bad condition*
Thermostat stuck or faulty	*Check and replace if necessary*
Ignition improperly timed	*Check and correct. Attend to possibly stuck advance mechanism*
Lean or rich mixture	*Check fuel system (see D)*
Excessive carbon desposit	*Decarbonize*
Obstructed exhaust system	*Check and repair or replace*
Cylinder-head gasket of the incorrect type	*Replace*